COUNTY GOVERNMENTS
IN AN
ERA OF CHANGE

Recent Titles in
Contributions in Political Science

COUNTY GOVERNMENTS IN AN ERA OF CHANGE

Edited by

David R. Berman

Contributions in Political Science,
Number 314
BERNARD K. JOHNPOLL,
Series Adviser

GREENWOOD PRESS
Westport, Connecticut • London

Library of Congress Cataloging-in-Publication Data

County governments in an era of change / edited by David R. Berman.
   p. cm. — (Contributions in political science, ISSN 0147–1066
; no. 314)
  Includes bibliographical references and index.
  ISBN 0–313–27824–5 (alk. paper)
   1. County government—United States. I. Berman, David R.
II. Series.
JS411.C726 1993
352′.0073—dc20   92–30013

British Library Cataloguing in Publication Data is available.

Library of Congress Catalog Card Number: 92–30013
ISBN: 0–313–27824–5
ISSN: 0147–1066

First published in 1993

Greenwood Press, 88 Post Road West, Westport, CT 06881
An imprint of Greenwood Publishing Group, Inc.

Printed in the United States of America

The paper used in this book complies with the
Permanent Paper Standard issued by the National
Information Standards Organization (Z39.48–1984).

10 9 8 7 6 5 4 3 2 1

Contents

Tables and Figures

TABLES

FIGURES

Preface

The inspiration for this book dates back to the discovery a few years ago that practitioners, journalists, and academics were beginning to pay considerable attention to county government. Exploration or reexploration of the "dark continent" of American politics was due to the growing role of counties as providers of services, both directly and in conjunction with other governments, and to the notion that counties were the next and perhaps the last frontier of local government. Noting the growing interest, I attempted to entice many of those most prominent in the new wave of inquiry to contribute to a book that would present a current assessment of county government. I am happy to report that there was considerable enthusiasm for this project and that a well-qualified group of contributors was more than willing to become involved. The following pages offer an assessment of county government that, we hope, will be of value to students of local government and intergovernmental relations, practitioners, and others concerned with changes taking place in the pattern of American government.

David R. Berman

Introduction

Counties, Change, and Reform: An Overview

David R. Berman and Katheryn A. Lehman

Observers have variously described county government in the United States as "the headless wonder," "the jungle of the American political scene," and "the dark continent of American government." The election of many executive "row" officers such as county assessor, attorney, sheriff, and treasurer, each of which is free to go his or her own way, makes the traditional county headless and formless. Using the jungle analogy, one author concluded several years ago: "In the county the law of the tooth and the claw seems to prevail, and only the fittest survive." Political activity, the author continued, takes place in the dense underbrush, away from the bright light of activity, where politicians "too often take advantage of the situation and work in devious and dishonest ways" (Van Petten, 1956, 205).

H. S. Gilbertson's (1917) famous description of counties as the "dark continent" further conveys the traditional image of a unit of government plagued by inefficiency, corruption, and lack of citizen respect and involvement. County governments have also been "dark" in the sense that scholars have left them largely unexplored.[1]

In recent years, however, both the public and the academic community have paid considerably more attention to county government. Much of this has had to do with the increased role played by counties as providers of urban services. Many counties are now providing on a regional basis functions and services once provided only by city governments. Along with changes in services and functions, many counties have become more centralized and streamlined in structure and better managed under the direction of professionally trained administrators.

Yet, while some counties are functioning much like city governments, one should also bear in mind that most counties do not function in this manner and there are important differences between most cities and most counties. Generally, counties have less discretion than cities in regard to such matters as revenue sources, structural arrangements, and what functions they can perform. Counties, unlike cities and towns, suffer something of an identity crisis, being, in effect, both units of local self-government and arms of the state government. On the operational level, county governments are far more likely than cities and towns to be headless and lack central direction. They are also more likely to be characterized by partisan politics.[2] On the output end, counties are more likely than cities to have responsibility for redistributive programs in such areas as welfare, public health, and hospitals.

County governments, over the years, have stimulated the imaginations of the reform-minded. Often, as one practice or reform idea becomes established, it is challenged by another. In successive waves of reform in the nineteenth and early twentieth centuries, counties were accused of not being democratic enough and, once changes were made, of suffering from an excess of democracy and the lack of managerial efficiency. Reformers of the Progressive Era in the early decades of the twentieth century did not get very far in their effort to shorten the county ballot or to upgrade the administration of county government. These demands, however, resurfaced in the current county reform movement, stimulated in large part by urbanization and suburbanization population trends that began after World War II and have intensified in recent years.

Buzzwords found in county reform efforts over the years are interrelated ideas of professionalization, modernization, and capacity improvement. Professionalism requires better training of officials (elected as well as appointed), recruitment based less on spoils and patronage and more on merit, and structural changes such as the county-manager system that place overall administrative responsibility in the hands of trained administrators. Modernization encompasses the above reforms but also includes the goal of giving counties more authority or home-rule power. Capacity-building refers to a variety of legal, fiscal, and administrative improvements that enhance the ability of counties to respond to citizen demands or to tasks required by state and federal law.

Counties generally have come a long way in all of the above respects. On the other hand, the persistence of traditional county arrangements and the wide diversity in the home rule authority, structure, and operation of county governments are striking. Reform, in short, has been uneven.

Reformers often point out that nonmetropolitan or rural county governments have the greatest need for reform, especially more professional and centralized management. Reformers view the lack of change or modernization as a barrier to performance. Citizens in many rural areas, on the other hand, appear to have little interest in change, particularly those calling for centralizing administration and reducing the number of elected officials. Residents in rural areas may feel that what they lose in terms of managerial efficiency by the fragmented system is more than offset by the positive effect the "long ballot" system has on accountability and governmental responsiveness (Weaver, 1992).

Overall, county governments in the United States are important, diverse, and changing. Counties increasingly grapple with enormous and vexing problems involving such matters as human services, the criminal justice system, and environmental protection. They are important in rural as well as urban and suburban areas as major units of general-purpose local government. At the same time, we should note that the responsibilities, operation, and structure of counties vary with the laws and customs of each state and with their location on a rural to urban continuum. Historically, counties have played a particularly important role in the South and West and a relatively unimportant role in New England. Generally, as suggested above, county governments in urban areas are more streamlined and active in the provision of services than those in rural areas.

The type and scope of problems facing county governments also vary considerably. The average population served by a county government is 71,465, but this ranges from around 100 in Loving County, Texas, to more than 8 million in Los Angeles County. Around 13 percent of all counties serve populations of 100,000 or more, but more than half serve communities under 25,000 in population (U.S. Bureau of the Census, 1988).

Some counties have experienced considerable growth, while others have faced declining populations and economic bases. In some large jurisdictions, getting the authority and dollars to keep up with growth has been a major problem. Rapidly growing Maricopa County, Arizona, for example, has an annual budget of more than $1.2 billion—about four times that of ten years ago, yet the Board of Supervisors cannot pass even a dog-leash ordinance without permission of the state legislature. At root, many of the problems in Maricopa County are financial in nature. As Betsey Bayless (1992), chair of the Maricopa County Board of Supervisors, put it in 1992: "Our revenues are down; our needs are up. Even as the economic downturn is giving us less; the public is demanding more."

Economic conditions in the early 1990s forced county officials in many urban areas to cope with huge deficits. In 1991, Montgomery and Prince George's counties in Maryland—a state somewhat unusual because counties include education spending in their budgets—ranked among the local governments, counting municipalities as well as counties, with the largest budget deficits (Norris, 1991). Economic stress has also been noticeable in many suburban and rural counties. Indeed, some of the more serious and persistent economic problems exist in rural counties. Regionally, counties in the South appear to have been under the greatest stress (Streib and Waugh, 1991b).

The ability of county governments to cope with their problems and build for the future depends greatly on intergovernmental arrangements. What county governments can do and how they may go about their tasks are set, in large part, by state law.[3] Reformers have long viewed state governments as obstacles to county progress. States have been reluctant to relinquish their control over counties and slow in equipping counties so that they can better respond to demands made on them. One should also quickly note, however, that mere grants of authority and other resources may not amount to much. Many counties have not taken advantage of state laws that allow them to frame and adopt their own charters. County officials, moreover, sometimes appear reluctant to exercise what powers they have.

County officials attempt to influence the policies of other governments by acting individually as lobbyists or through groups such as county associations at the state level and the National Association of Counties (NACo) at the national level. County officials at times, over the years, have enjoyed considerable success with state and federal legislatures (Wright, 1988; Haider, 1974). In recent years, as economic times have become tougher, however, state legislators and members of Congress have tended to regard county spokespersons as special pleaders who engage in "poor mouthing"—the practice of claiming "that you don't have anything, can't get anything, and have no hope for the future" (Bragg, 1988, 2).

Currently high on the wish list for county officials is the establishment or reestablishment of strong partnerships with state governments and the national government. Partnerships mean greater county input in shaping state and federal programs and more state and federal financial assistance to help counties meet citizen demands. They also mean a reduction in mandates imposed on counties by state and federal laws and regulations. Requirements that counties undertake specific functions, ranging from solid waste protection and growth controls to health care, may distort local priorities, impose tasks beyond the capabilities of county governments, and require large expenditures of locally raised funds.

Partnerships with higher levels of government, particularly the national government, have been difficult to establish in recent years. Counties, however, have been much more successful in entering into various types of cooperative endeavors with other units of local government. Indeed, counties often are central elements in the network of local government, directly providing essential areawide services and working with other units under contracts and agreements and through such organizations as councils of government. Interlocal cooperation increases the capacities of the units involved and improves the provision of services, often on a metropolitan or regional basis.

The following pages elaborate on the basic themes we have set forth in this Introduction regarding the past, present, and future of county governments and their structure, operation, services, problems, and ties to other governments. In pursuing the general topic of change and reform, we look at counties as: (1) units of local government evolving over time as the result of various forces; (2) governmental entities with varying powers, structures, procedures, and performance levels; (3) service providers in different settings, varying along rural-urban lines; and (4) participants in patterns of intergovernmental politics characterized by both competition and cooperation.

Lawrence Martin opens the discussion with an analysis of how county governments in the United States have been molded and shaped by various historical influences. These include the English shire system, colonial settlement patterns, Jacksonian Democracy, nineteenth-century court decisions, and the Progressive Movement. Martin argues that these influences have left traditions and tensions that continue to affect the functioning and role of county governments. Martin also notes the forces behind the current era of concern with county government and some of the effects of the contemporary reform effort.

Many of the points made in Chapter 1 are elaborated in subsequent chapters. The various authors turn out to have somewhat different ideas about the overall status and future evolution of county governments. Some are impressed by the changes made and find counties well on their way to becoming "the local government of the 1990s" (Chapter 5). Others are less impressed by the current level of county performance and see the need for greater reform—be it professionalism, modernization, capacity-building—so that counties can respond to the new demands upon them. Still others suggest the possibility that regional governments, encompassing more than one county, rather than county governments, will be the local governments of the future (Chapter 10).

Chapters 2, 3, and 4 examine counties as governmental entities—their authority, structure, operation, and performance. Victor DeSantis and Tari Renner in Chapter 2 examine county home rule and how county discretion in regard to such matters as finance, structure, and functions differs from state to state. The authors go on to examine different forms of government and types of electoral systems found on the county level. Counties are divided into three basic structural types: the traditional commission form and the more modern county administrator and county executive forms. While reformers and practitioners have definite ideas about which of these forms is best, we know very little about the actual effects of employing different systems. Nor do we know much about the effects of various electoral arrangements and voting systems. We do know from the DeSantis and Renner chapter that the selection of county legislators raises important questions, often brought before the courts, in regard to redistricting and representation.

Among the major formal actors in county politics are county legislators known by such names as commissioners, supervisors, freeholders, and even judges. County legislators, Alvin Sokolow notes in Chapter 3, have much in common with city council members. Yet they also differ in that they must somehow make peace with a host of independent executives (the row officers), typically have less staff assistance at their disposal, and function in what is often an intensely partisan atmosphere. Conflict is no stranger to county legislators—being manifest in disputes along urban-rural as well as partisan lines and frequently occurring over the allocation of services and expenditures. Sokolow brings us closer to the work world of the county legislator. He also raises the question of whether county legislatures have changed over the last 30 years. He finds some change, but not much. County legislators, in particular, still operate primarily as administrators rather than policy-makers and, at best, are only reluctant policy innovators.[4]

William Waugh and Gregory Streib in Chapter 4 also concern themselves with the question of just how much county governments have changed. More directly they ask whether counties have the capacities of a fiscal, political, and administrative nature to respond to problems brought to them by citizens or state and federal mandates. Not surprisingly, they find great variation: "There are some counties delivering the most demanding services very effectively, and there are counties operating literally out of the garages and checkbooks of elected officials with little regard for fiscal accountability." Can they do the job? Survey research conducted by the authors suggests that county officials seem to think so. But these officials also feel that they need certain types of help, mostly of a financial nature, from the state and federal governments.

County services and the urban-rural setting of county government are explored in Chapters 5, 6, and 7. In Chapter 5 J. Edwin Benton and Donald C. Menzel examine the growing service of counties in general. They conclude that urbanization, suburbanization, and modernization have severely reduced the gap between counties and cities in terms of service responsibilities. County governments, particularly in urban areas, have become big businesses and full-service governments. Urban counties are becoming much more like their municipal counterparts in providing services such as police and fire protection, emergency medical care, water service, and environmental protection. In states like Florida, the authors point out, counties have become particularly important in providing services in rapidly growing unincorporated areas.

Vincent L. Marando and C. Douglas Baker in Chapter 6 echo some of these themes in pointing out how metropolitan areas are being transformed away from a dominant core and, with this, how counties have taken on increasingly important roles in policy-making and service delivery. They review the general landscape of metropolitan growth in light of 1990 census figures and look at different categories of counties as defined by their population size and spatial relationship to the central city. They follow this with an analysis of county services, both top-tier and bottom-tier, in metropolitan areas. Metropolitan counties, the authors emphasize, play an important function in providing redistributive programs. The authors also see metropolitan counties faced with growing problems of financing capital projects and paying off debts. The last section of the chapter makes the point that the role of counties in metropolitan areas is vitally affected by county-state relations, home-rule status, and the nature of the local government network.

Rural counties are of concern to Beverly Cigler, who begins Chapter 7 by pointing out the importance of rural communities in American life and the problems faced by such communities and the governments that serve them. Among the problems are economic decline, out-migration, poverty, lack of amenities, and underfunded governmental services. Cigler introduces us to different types of rural communities as determined, in part, by their economic base and population characteristics. County governments in rural areas are, the author notes, often the dominant general purpose local governments. Compared to counties in metropolitan areas, counties in rural areas are less likely to have home-rule status, more likely to have the traditional government structure, and more likely to play the traditional role of administrative arm of the state, although many provide urban-like services to unincorporated areas. In this chapter we return to the capacity problem and, in particular, to capacity-building aid for rural governments offered by the states.

The final three chapters of the book turn to intergovernmental relations. County-state relations are covered in Chapter 8 by Tanis J. Salant, who examines how directors of county associations view relations with state legislatures, governors, administrators, and courts. Salant's research provides insights into the quality of these relationships, some of the attitudes that underlie them, and their outcomes. She finds that association directors generally consider their relations with the legislature to be positive, though this has more to do with the access, trust, and respect they receive than with what the legislature actually does for counties in terms of funding or programs. Association directors also view relations with governors and administrators as generally favorable, while they give courts mixed reviews. In her concluding section, Salant touches upon the current and potential influence of counties in state capitals. Several of those interviewed felt that legislators treated them less like a valued partner and more like a special interest—no different than the "tavern association" or "tobacco lobby." The notion of a partnership, however, appears to be gaining some ground. Similarly, Salant's work suggests that county officials may be at the beginning of a long-term shift away from a basically passive and subservient attitude toward state officials.

David Berman and Barbara Greene follow the discussion of counties in state politics by focusing on the county agenda in national politics. In Chapter 9 Berman and Greene look at the history of federal activity involving counties and other units of local government and at the world of public interest groups that form the intergovernmental lobby in Washington, D.C. Considerable attention is given to the policies and policy objectives of the National Association of Counties, which is the only national organization representing counties. The chapter considers NACo's varied program objectives, ranging from urban housing and health services to agricultural policies and activities. The authors show that while public interest groups like NACo have lost considerable influence in Washington in recent years, they have not given up on the restoration of the federal-local partnership.

The final chapter by David Berman looks at counties as functioning in an unstable environment in which governments continually bump into each other. The author examines counties as part of a network or system of local governments—an international relations analogy is found useful in this respect—and as part of a vertical system in which they interact with the federal and state governments. Counties are expected to play several roles over the next decade: as direct providers of services, as partners in interjurisdictional arrangements, and as agents of the state. The author concludes that how well counties will play these roles depends on the assistance of other governments, their fiscal health, and perhaps most importantly, on the willingness of county officials to take the initiative in exercising their authority and in building their capacities.

NOTES

1. Among the pioneer works on counties are Wager (1950), Duncombe (1977), and Bollens et al. (1969).

2. Political party organizations are alive and well in the counties (Cotter et al., 1984; Frendreis, Gibson, and Vertz, 1990). Party ties have much to do with who gets elected to county office. Partisan conflicts also characterize the operation of county governing bodies (see Sokolow, Chapter 3 in this book).

3. Existing research on the subject suggests that the variation among states in regard to how much discretion they give counties is partially explained by a combination of historical, cultural, demographic, and managerial variables (Berman and Martin, 1988).

4. Other scholars have noted that in many counties much of the gap in policy leadership has been filled by professionally trained county managers who generally operate behind the scenes (Nalbandian, 1990).

COUNTY GOVERNMENTS
IN AN
ERA OF CHANGE

Chapter 1

American County Government: An Historical Perspective

Lawrence L. Martin

Like many of our governmental institutions, American county government has been molded and shaped by historical influences. In order to appreciate fully the structure, functions, financing, politics, and intergovernmental relations of American county government today, it is necessary to understand the historical antecedents that have influenced it. American county government has largely been shaped by six major historical influences: (1) English county government, (2) American colonial settlement patterns, (3) the frontier spirit and the democratization of American county government, (4) nineteenth-century state court decisions, (5) the Progressive Era and the government reform movement, and (6) the post-World War II urbanization of the suburbs. Each of these historical influences created certain tensions in American county government; most of these tensions still remain unresolved today. Thus, the past continues to influence the present, and most likely the future, of American county government.

ENGLISH COUNTY GOVERNMENT

American county government traces its family tree back nearly 1,000 years to the old English shire. In the ninth century, the Kingdom of England was divided by royal decree into governmental districts called "shires." The governmental structure of a shire consisted of a shire court, which possessed both judicial and legislative powers, and three shire officials: the earl, the sheriff, and the bishop, who shared the executive power (Fairlie, 1906; Goche, 1987).

The principal governmental functions performed by the shire included the administration of the police and military functions, the operation of the court system, public works, poor relief, and taxation (Fairlie and Kneier, 1930). The shire court was comprised of 12 landholders who assembled periodically to enact ordinances and to pass judgment on criminal and civil complaints brought by citizens.

The shire was presided over by an earl, usually a large landholder, appointed by the king. The earl was also in charge of military personnel stationed in the shire. Next in importance to the earl was the shire-reeve, the forerunner of the modern county sheriff. The shire-reeve, or sheriff, served as the steward of the royal estates, the tax collector, and president of the shire court in all nonecclesiastical matters. The bishop replaced the sheriff as president of the shire court when church-related issues were dealt with (Fairlie, 1906, 6).

The *de jure* legal status of the shire was that of an administrative district, or arm, of the crown. However, the crown granted most of its shire officers a great deal of discretion in deciding local matters (Webb and Webb, 1906). As a result, the shire also functioned *de facto* as a unit of local government.

After the Norman Conquest of England in 1066, the shire was reconstituted as a county, and the powers of the earl and bishop were greatly reduced. The position of earl was relegated to the status of mere title of nobility. The bishop, as a result of the separation of church and state affairs, was removed entirely from county affairs. The decline in the power of the earl and bishop resulted in the sheriff emerging as the preeminent county official.

The sheriff maintained his position as the supreme county official until the fourteenth century. During this period, King Edward III became dissatisfied with the concentration of county executive authority in a single official. This concern led to the creation by royal decree of a new county official, the justice of the peace. At least one justice of the peace was appointed for each county, while some counties had anywhere from 20 to 60 depending upon their population and geographical size (Fairlie & Kneier, 1930). The justices of the peace were assigned many of the duties and responsibilities previously belonging to the sheriff. Later additional county officers, such as the coroner and the constable, were also established. With the addition of each new county officer, the executive power of county government became more pluralized.

Three aspects of English county government have particular relevance for an understanding of American county government today. First, the blending of the county judicial and legislative powers in the county court demonstrated a general lack of concern for the separation of powers doctrine. While this doctrine is a cornerstone of the U.S. Constitution and the constitutions of the 50 states, the doctrine was not established in the structure of English county government. This lack of concern with the separation of powers doctrine became a legacy that was passed along to American county government.

For the most part, American county government structure still demonstrates a lack of concern with the separation of powers doctrine. The overlap today, however, is between the executive and legislative powers rather than between the judicial and legislative.

The second major English influence that has had a lasting effect on American county government is the preference for dividing the county executive function among multiple county officers. This pluralization of the executive power is frequently identified as a significant problem in determining accountability and control in the administration of county affairs.

The third major English influence on American county government is the *de jure* legal status of the county as an administrative arm of the state and its *de facto* status as a unit of local government. These two different conceptualizations of American county government continue to create tensions and generate problems today. As an arm of state government, American county government has only marginal capability for independent policy-making and action. As a unit of local government, however, citizens look to American county government to respond to local service needs brought about by growth and urbanization.

COLONIAL SETTLEMENT PATTERNS

When the American colonies were being established, the need obviously arose for some type of local government. Some of the first settlements, like the Massachusetts Bay Colony, created compacts, or contracts, which consisted of rules that the colonists mutually agreed would govern them in their new communities. As the number of colonists increased and as the geographical size of the colonies expanded, the need arose for more formalized local government structures. The form of local government chosen was largely determined by the different colonial settlement patterns in the northern, southern, and middle colonies.

In the northern colonies, the original colonists tended to cluster in small closely knit communities for protection against the Indians and for other forms of social support. A general rule of thumb at the time was that no colonist should live more than one-half mile from the community meeting house (Bollens, 1978, 190). As a result of this pattern of settlement, towns were the first units of local government formed in the northern colonies.

In the southern colonies, the English manorial system was adopted. This settlement pattern led to the creation of large working farms called plantations and the dispersion of the original colonists over vast geographical areas. In the southern colonies, the county became the principal form of local government simply because it was the proper English governmental unit to serve a large geographical area.

The first American county governments were established in Virginia in 1634. The Commonwealth of Virginia was divided into eight counties that became the basic administrative districts of the state. Members of the colonial assembly were elected on the basis of counties. Counties also served as state military, judicial, public works, and taxation districts, much as they had in England (Fairlie and Kneier, 1930, 13).

Like its English ancestor, the original governing body of Virginia's counties was the county court, whose members were large landholders appointed by the colonial governor. The sheriff was the principal county executive officer serving as president of the court, tax collector, and county treasurer. The sheriff did not, however, possess the totality of the county executive power. In keeping with the tradition of English county government, the Virginia county executive power was pluralized among several county officers. In addition to appointing a sheriff for each Virginia county, the royal governor also appointed a coroner, a surveyor, a lieutenant, and multiple justices of the peace (Duncombe, 1977, 21).

The first northern county governments were established in the Massachusetts Bay Colony in 1643. Structurally, Massachusetts county government was quite similar to that of Virginia. The governing body of a Massachusetts county was again the county court. The royal governor of Massachusetts also appointed a sheriff and a treasurer for each county, thus maintaining the plural executive function. Massachusetts county government officers were fewer in number than in Virginia, due principally to the fact that cities and towns were considered more important units of local government. Having been created prior to counties, Massachusetts cities and towns performed many of the duties and functions that counties handled in Virginia.

The middle colonies of Pennsylvania, New York, and New Jersey developed their own unique county government permutations. The differences were primarily related to the structure and election of the county governing body. In New York and New Jersey, as in the New England colonies, cities and towns were the principal local government units. Unlike the New England colonies, however, when counties were constituted in New York and New Jersey, the unit of electoral representation became the city or town. For example, in New York, one member of the county governing board, called the board of supervisors, was elected from each ward of a city and each town supervisor served as an ex-officio member. Likewise in New Jersey, two freeholders were elected from each city and township in the county and served as the county governing board called a board of "chosen freeholders" (Effross, 1975, 1). Through this structural arrangement, the municipal officials of New York and New Jersey attempted to insure that cities and towns would maintain a primacy vis-a-vis counties.

County government in Pennsylvania took a different path than in New York and New Jersey. Pennsylvania was an anomaly because county government was consciously established as the principal unit of local government. The reason for Pennsylvania's atypical approach was William Penn. In deciding upon a form of local government for Pennsylvania, Penn simply preferred counties (Aderlfer, 1975, 5). Penn consequently established Philadelphia, Bucks, and Chester counties in 1682.

Because of the absence of any competitive positioning between county government and cities and towns in Pennsylvania, intergovernmental considerations did not play a part in determining the unit of representation for the election of the county governing board as it had in New York and New Jersey. Pennsylvania chose the citizenry, rather than cities and towns, as the unit of representation for election of members to its governing boards called commissions. County commissions were composed of three commissioners elected "at large" by the enfranchised citizens residing in the county.

In summary, colonial settlement patterns were influential on the development of American county government because they preordained that counties would be relatively weak units of government in the Northeast, relatively strong units in the South, and somewhat mixed units in the middle states. Colonial settlement patterns and the approaches to county government they engendered were ultimately dispersed and diffused throughout different parts of the country. The limited Massachusetts form of county government spread to most of the other colonies in New England, while the strong Virginia form of county government diffused throughout the southern colonies. The structure of the county governing board in New York and New Jersey eventually spread to Ohio, Michigan, Wisconsin, and Illinois. The Pennsylvania form of county government, with its county commissioners elected at large, eventually diffused throughout most of the western United States (Kajfez, Hall, and Karnig, 1984, 3–4).

THE FRONTIER SPIRIT AND THE DEMOCRATIZATION OF AMERICAN COUNTY GOVERNMENT

As settlers moved west from the original colonial states, opened up new lands and created new communities, new units of local government and new governmental structures were also needed. The newly emerging frontier states tended to simply import their governmental structures from the older more established colonial states—with one major exception. The frontier states preferred to elect rather than appoint their government officials.

During the American colonial period as well as the early years of our national experience, county officials tended to be appointed rather than elected. The appointments were usually the sole prerogatives of the colonial governors and later the state governors. This system of appointing county officials tended to maintain in power a conservative elite minority of wealthy and influential individuals and families. Jacksonian Democracy and the "frontier spirit" was characterized by egalitarianism and an abiding suspicion of aristocratic cliques and expertise. In order to make government more accessible to the common man, the frontier spirit found expression in a generalized demand for the direct election of government officials including county officials (Duncombe, 1977, 23).

The number of elected county officers in the newly formed State of Indiana is indicative of the democratizing influence of the frontier spirit on American county government. The first Indiana state constitution, adopted in 1816, called for the election in each county of a board of county commissioners, an auditor, a recorder, a treasurer, a surveyor, a clerk of the court, a sheriff, and a coroner (Fairlie, 1906, 37; Duncombe, 1977, 23). In the same vein, the State of Illinois' first constitution called for the election of a board of county commissioners, a sheriff, a coroner, a recorder, clerks of the court, and justices of the peace (Fairlie, 1906, 37). Mississippi made county constables, justices of the peace, and probate judges elective officials in 1832. Tennessee followed suit in 1834 with county clerks, sheriffs, justices of the peace, and constables (Fairlie, 1906, 40).

The influence of the frontier spirit on American county government was also felt in some of the older established states. New York State, for example, made a number of previously appointed county officers elected positions in 1821. Delaware made county sheriffs and coroners elected positions in 1831. New York, Massachusetts, and New Hampshire extended the election idea to cover district attorneys and judges (Gilbertson,

1917, 29). Even Pennsylvania felt a touch of the frontier spirit and made the position of county sheriff elective in 1838 (Fairlie, 1906, 40; Duncombe, 1977, 23). Rhode Island was a singular exception to the movement to elect county officials, as it continued to appoint the majority of its county officials including sheriffs (Gilbertson, 1917, 29). Rhode Island eventually abolished organized county government in 1842.

By calling for the direct election of county officials, the frontier spirit brought about the democratization of American county government while contributing to and extending the English notion of the pluralization of the executive power. The average county today is still characterized by a number of independently elected officials sharing the county's executive power.

NINETEENTH-CENTURY COURT DECISIONS

The middle 1800s represent an important turning point for American county government. Up to this time, many county governments had functioned as both administrative arms of the state and as units of local government, in much the same ways that counties had acted in England and during the colonial period. During the middle 1800s, the formal legal status of American county government was clarified for the first time. The judicial decisions handed down during this era established the legal precedents that would be cited, and that are still cited today, in determining the legal status and powers of American county government. Three cases decided during this period are worth specific mention due to their subsequent judicial influence.

In 1845 the U.S. Supreme Court was called upon to determine the legal status and powers of its county government in the case of *State of Maryland v. Baltimore and Ohio Railroad.* Chief Justice Taney, writing for the court, stated in part that "counties are nothing more than certain potions of the territory into which the state is divided for the more convenient exercise of the powers of government" (Duncombe, 1977, 23). Chief Justice Taney's decision followed closely the English principle that counties were primarily administrative districts of the state.

In 1857 the Ohio Supreme Court likewise found itself confronted with the task of determining the legal status and powers of Ohio county governments. In a decision handed down in the case of *Commissioners of Hamilton County v. Mighels,* the Ohio Supreme court followed closely the Taney decision in stating that

A municipal corporation proper is created mainly for the interest, advantage, and convenience of the locality and its people; a county organization is created almost exclusively with a view to the policy of the state at large, for purposes of political organization and civil administration, in matters of finance, of education, of provision for the poor, of military organization, of the means of travel and transport, and especially for the general adminis- tration of justice. With scarcely an exception, all the powers and functions of the county organization have a direct and exclusive reference to the general policy of the state and are, in fact, but a branch of the general administration of that policy (Duncombe, 1977, 19).

Another important case that significantly affected the emerging doctrine concerning the legal status of American county government was the 1868 Iowa case of *Merriam v. Moody's Executors*. In deciding this case, Justice John F. Dillon of the Iowa Supreme Court wrote that the powers of local governments were governed by three rules: (1) municipal governments had only those powers expressly delegated to them by the state legislature in their enabling legislation, (2) those powers necessary and incident to execution of the express powers, and (3) those powers absolutely neces- sary to discharge the express powers (Facwett, 1986).

The Iowa decision was the most influential in terms of subsequent impact on the legal status of American county government. While essen- tially a decision relating to municipal government, the impact of the ruling was extended to county governments as well. "Dillon's Rule," as the decision came to be known, was in keeping with the previous decisions that counties were exclusively administrative arms of the state, or "quasi- corporations," having only those powers expressly delegated by the state or necessarily implied to discharge the powers expressly delegated. Dillon's Rule meant that counties had to have specific enabling state legislation in order to function as units of local government. Dillon's Rule also meant that counties could respond to the changing needs of their citizens only by petitioning their state legislatures for specific grants of additional authority that might, or might not, be granted.

Limiting the ability of American county government to function as a unit of local government probably was not seen as a major problem in the middle 1800s. Counties were looked upon as primarily rural forms of government. When American county governments encountered the mod- ern suburbanization movement beginning after World War II, however, their inability to function as units of local government would eventually create major service delivery problems.

THE PROGRESSIVE ERA AND THE
GOVERNMENT REFORM MOVEMENT

The Progressive Era, which can be dated roughly from the turn of the century until about 1920, was a period of general concern for government reform, particularly at the state and local levels. At the time, political bosses ruled many of the country's largest local governments. Graft, corruption, nepotism, and the spoils system characterized many municipal and county governments. Because American county government was less well understood by the citizenry than was municipal government, some reformers believed the corruption in county government was even more insidious. In 1917 H. S. Gilbertson authored a particularly influential book during this period called *The County: The "Dark Continent" of American Politics*. The title captured the essence of the reformers' views of American county government.

In response to the belief that local government in general, and county government in specific, needed to be "reformed," organizations such as the National Municipal League (now the National Civic League) and the National Short Ballot Organization undertook the task of bringing about change. These organizations, frequently created, financed, and directed by business leaders, put forth numerous reform concepts. Four of these reforms had particular import for the development of American county government: (1) the abolition of the fee system; (2) a return to the appointment, rather than election, of most county officials; (3) the professionalization of county government; and (4) home rule.

Rather then being paid a fixed salary like their municipal counterparts, many county officials derived their compensation primarily, or exclusively, from fees, fines, penalties, and permits. This approach to the compensation of county officials was dubbed the "fee system," and it constituted an open invitation to abuse. For example, the sheriff of New York County reportedly collected and retained in one year alone (1916) some $60,000 in fees, while the Cook County (Illinois) treasurer is reported to have pocketed nearly $500,000 in fees during a four-year term in office. When, as part of an investigation, the Cook County treasurer declined to disclose what had happened to the half million dollars in fees he had collected, Illinois state statutes governing the fee system protected his right to silence (Gilbertson, 1917, 51).

The Progressive Era reformers were also firm in their belief that too many county officials were elected. The reformers charged that the election of so many county officials created a situation in which no one was really in charge of county government. The democratization of American county government, the reformers charged, had actually led to a situation that was inherently "undemocratic" (Fairlie and Kneier, 1930, 107).

The reformers wanted fewer elected, and more appointed, county officials with a resulting shorter election ballot. Gilbertson, writing in 1917 for the National Short Ballot Organization, put the argument against the direct election of the majority of county officials thusly: "For nearly a century popular government has been galloping down the highway that leads to government confusion. No where does the record state that because the people elected long strings of officials, the people therefore controlled those officials" (p. 31).

Yet another Progressive Era reform idea was the notion that municipal and county governments should be professionally managed. Business and community leaders looked at the organization and management of county government and were dismayed by what they saw. An Ohio commission appointed to study county government in the early 1920s concluded in its report that "in administrative organization county government presents a picture of extraordinary complexity . . . [and] . . . violates almost every principle of business and governmental organization which experience has evolved" (Fairlie and Kneier, 1930, 43).

Organizations like the National Municipal League and the New York Bureau of Municipal Research were instrumental during this period in promoting the idea of professional training for local government administrators. These organizations also advocated alterations in the structure of American county government to provide for the council/manager form of government. Under the council/manager plan, a county administrator position would be imposed between the elected governing board and the county bureaucracy. The elected officials would concentrate on policy; the county administrator would handle the administration and be guided by the goals of efficiency and productivity. In 1927, Iredell County, North Carolina, became the first county in the nation to adopt the council/administrator form (Zeller, 1975, 28). The county administrator form is one of the three major forms in use today (see Cahpter 2 of this volume).

County government reforms introduced during the Progressive Era met with mixed success overall. The reformers won virtually a complete victory over the fee system. While counties still collect a variety of fees today, most county officials (both elected and appointed) are salaried, with their compensation unrelated to fees. When it comes to the notions of appointment versus election of county officials and the professionalization of American county government administration, however, only partial successes have been registered to date (see Chapter 4). The pluralization of the county executive function remains the modal form of American county government and only a minority of American counties have professionalized their administrative structures by creation of a county administrator position (DeSantis, 1989).

As part of their overall strategy to promote the appointment of county officials and to encourage the professionalization of American county government, Progressive Era reformers also advocated "home rule" for American county government. Home rule is one of those nebulous concepts that tends to defy exact definition. Broadly interpreted, however, home rule can be thought of as the grant by state legislatures to county governments of general powers that enable them to act more like units of local government and less like administrative arms of the state. Los Angeles County, California, became the first American county government to adopt a charter in 1913.

POST-WORLD WAR II URBANIZATION OF THE SUBURBS

Because of their legal status as an administrative arm of the state, American county governments were simply not adequately prepared to respond to the service demands created by the suburbanization movement that began after World War II. Even though the new suburban citizens moved into unincorporated areas, they expected—and demanded—the same government services they had enjoyed in the cities. Now, however, they looked to county government to provide them. The suburbanization movement began to blur the distinction between the functions and services municipalities had traditionally provided and those traditionally provided by counties. A 1952 study identified a number of new functions and services being provided by counties: public health, hospitals, fire protection, libraries, housing, utilities, and parks and recreation (Snider 1952).

In attempting to provide the new myriad services demanded by suburbanites, county governments faced new problems and new tensions. County government found itself placed in the position of acting like a unit of local government but without the legal power. Non-home-rule counties were forced to appeal constantly to their state legislatures for grants of additional authority to respond to the increasing service demands of their citizens. A large number of the bills introduced into state legislatures each year dealt with specific county issues for which American county government lacked the authority to deal.

The problems of responding to the service demands created by suburbanization without being able to function as a unit of local government spawned the county modernization movement. The term "county modernization" refers broadly to the abandonment of the traditional model of county government with its distinguishing characteristics: as an administrative arm of the state, performing state-mandated functions and services, and with its pluralized executive, or commission, form of government (Duncombe, 1977, 29). In order to promote county modernization, proponents again focused on the issue of county home rule.

County home rule generally takes one of two forms. The broadest grant of home-rule powers are conferred by state legislatures to "charter" county governments. A charter is essentially a miniconstitution approved by the citizens of the county. Under a charter, counties have broad grants of discretionary authority to alter the functions and services they provide; change their organizational structure; add, delete, and change personnel; and to levy and raise taxes without seeking additional grants of discretionary authority from state legislatures (Berman and Martin, 1988). A more restricted grant of home rule powers is referred to as the "optional form." Under the optional form, counties are permitted some discretionary authority in selecting the form of county government they believe best suits their needs, but remain restricted in the areas of structural, personnel, and fiscal discretionary authority (T. Salant, 1988, 8–10).

By the end of the 1950s, only 11 states had granted their counties home rule, either charter or optional form (T. Salant, 1988a, 18). By the end of the 1980s, 36 of the 48 states with county governments (Rhode Island and Connecticut have none) provided for some form of home rule; 23 of these states permitted counties to adopt a charter (DeSantis, 1989, 56). The total number of states currently allowing charter adoption is 24 (see Chapter 2).

The demographic shift to the suburbs and the county modernization movement created a host of intergovernmental tensions that most American county governments had not previously encountered. The provision of urban or municipal-type services transformed many county governments into regional service delivery agencies and frequently brought them into direct competition and conflict with cities and towns over which level of government should provide what services to what citizens. Likewise, demands for county home rule frequently put counties at odds with municipalities and state legislatures because the state-local government balance of power would be altered (Berman, Martin, and Kajfez, 1985). Attempting to determine the proper role and responsibilities of county government in the local intergovernmental context remains a major unresolved issue.

CONCLUSION

American county government is the product of the interplay of various historical influences, each of which created tensions concerning the nature and proper role of American county government. In turn, these tensions affected the growth and evolution of American county government.

Specific tensions identified in this chapter include the differing conceptualizations of counties as administrative arms of the state and as units of local government; the pluralization of the county executive function; the blurring and blending of the legislative, judicial, and executive functions; the regional variations in the powers, structures, and functions of counties; and the issue of elected versus appointed county officials. The continuing influence of these unresolved tensions is remarked upon in the following chapters.

Chapter 2

Governing the County: Authority, Structure, and Elections

Victor S. DeSantis and Tari Renner

County governments in the United States vary in their responsibilities, authority, and basic structures. Their election systems, though heavily partisan in comparison to those found in most cities and towns, also vary considerably. How much responsibility and home-rule authority counties should have, what forms of government counties should adopt, and how counties should structure their election systems are hotly debated questions. Moving from the past, this chapter presents a brief discussion of the responsibilities of counties (more is said about this in the following chapter) and proceeds to consider questions concerning the nature and significance of variations in county authority, different forms of county government, and different types of election or voting systems.

RESPONSIBILITIES

Counties have gradually emerged during this century as major providers of a wide range of governmental services. They continue to provide the traditional functions of property tax assessment and collection, recording of deeds, law enforcement, county jails, public works, welfare and social services, health services, and agricultural functions. At the same time, it has become increasingly common for counties to be involved in more urban and optional services such as housing, mass transit, highways, airports, parks and recreation, water supply and sewage, planning, zoning, and regional governance.

The functional responsibilities of counties depend substantially on state law and their population size and metropolitan status. The largest and most urban counties tend to perform the widest range of services. This is particularly the case for urban service functions such as transportation, community development, legal services, parks and recreation, and cultural activities (Duncombe, 1977, 20).

Recent research by Mark Schneider and Kee Ok Park (1989) has found that metropolitan counties actually perform more services than suburban municipalities. In constructing an index across the 31 functional categories used in the 1982 Census of Governments, they found urban counties involved in an average of 14.0 different services compared to 10.5 for suburban cities. This gap was especially wide for redistributive (social welfare) functions. The cities perform more services of a developmental nature than did counties, but this difference was much narrower than it had been a decade earlier.

The distribution of county expenditures for fiscal year 1988–89 is presented in Figure 2.1. As the figure indicates, social service and income maintenance programs, such as health and hospitals (15.9%), public welfare (13.7%), and education (13.9%), remain the dominant service areas of county government. However, certain trends over the past decade reflect gradual shifts in county service delivery. The 1980s witnessed a decrease in the percentage of county expenditures on social services and an increase in the percentage spent in areas such as public safety, highways, and debt maintenance. While these trends are by no means dramatic, they are another indication of the changing nature of county government from a more traditional to a more diverse service unit.

COUNTY HOME RULE

As counties have acquired more functions in response to greater service demands, a gradual trend has developed toward granting them greater autonomy and flexibility in their policy-making and administrative activities. In 1952, Clyde Snider maintained that county dependence on state institutions was a "major obstacle in the path of county progress" (p. 74). Greater local autonomy or self-governance is accomplished through home rule or optional charters. At the time of Snider's work, only 6 states granted counties the opportunity to establish such charters. Further, in these states only 12 counties out of a possible universe of about 200 had actually adopted home-rule charters.

Historically, the movement toward greater local autonomy and home-rule charters has come much slower for counties than for cities. This is not to suggest, however, that all states have moved at a constant pace or in the same

Figure 2.1
Percentage Distribution of Total County Expenditures, 1988–89 (total: $119.3 billion)

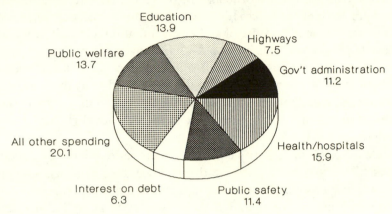

Education
13.9

Highways
7.5

Public welfare
13.7

Gov't administration
11.2

All other spending
20.1

Health/hospitals
15.9

Interest on debt
6.3

Public safety
11.4

Source: U.S. Bureau of the Census.

direction. Texas, for example, was one of the first states to grant county home rule, in 1933, and the only state to revoke the provision, in 1969. This had little impact on Texas counties, however, since not one of them had adopted a home-rule charter during those 36 years that the provision was in effect.

The overall pace of home rule during the last century is reflected in the priorities and activities of local government reformers. A *Model County Charter* was finally published by the National Civic League (at the time, the National Municipal League) in 1956, with the only revision coming in 1990. In contrast, the first *Model City Charter* was published by the League in 1900 and was revised for the seventh time in 1989.

As indicated in Chapter 1, currently, among the 48 states with county governments, 36 grant them some form of home-rule authority. Of those 36 states, 24 offer counties the ability to adopt a home-rule charter, while 12 offer them a more narrow grant of authority through limited home-rule or optional forms of government. As recently as 1965, only 18 states permitted the choice of either form. The movement toward county home rule reached a peak from 1972 to 1974, when 9 states passed such provisions. These changes, however, have not brought about dramatic changes in county operation. Only 117 of the 1,307 eligible counties have succeeded in adopting some form of home rule (T. Salant, 1988a, 10). Therefore, over 95 percent of American counties (about 2,924 of 3,042) remain general law counties subject to almost unlimited state control.

The ability to draft and adopt a home-rule charter is a necessary but not sufficient condition for counties to garner local discretionary authority. For many reasons, county officials are often ambivalent about moving toward greater independence. It has also been suggested that some local officials are frequently unsure of and hesitant to test their authority under home-rule provisions. This may be due to the overly vague and complex nature of state provisions or a bit of caution by local officials, especially in light of court decisions that have gradually chipped away the "sovereign immunity" of local governments. Other local officials may remain more interested in passing the political buck to the state level (U.S. Advisory Commission, 1981, 60).

While the scope of authority under home rule varies widely by state, the powers have often been categorized into three general areas: structure, functional responsibility, and fiscal administration. In a study of local discretionary authority looking into these three areas, as well as personnel administration, the U.S. Advisory Commission on Intergovernmental Relations (ACIR) developed composite indexes of local authority for cities, counties, and other types of local governments. The concluding observation of the report was that "in most states general purpose governments in fact do fall short of possessing broad structural, functional, and financing powers—particularly the last" (U.S. Advisory Commission, 1981, 60).

Table 2.1 shows the composite rankings of city and county discretionary authority by state. The greatest degree of county discretionary authority across the four dimensions is granted by Oregon, Alaska (which refers to counties as boroughs), North Carolina, Pennsylvania, and Delaware. While some states like North Carolina and Oregon offer similar levels of autonomy to both cities and counties, other states differentiate substantially in the level of autonomy offered to the different types of local government. For example, Texas and Missouri, which rank very high in the degree of discretionary authority offered to cities, fall to the bottom in the ranking for counties. All 254 Texas counties are constitutionally mandated to operate under the commission form of government with a county judge elected at-large and four commissioners elected by districts. This system is used in counties as large and diverse as Harris County (almost 2.9 million population), which includes Houston and its suburbs, and in Loving County, with a population of 100 (Kraemer and Newell, 1990, 57).

In the structural area, home rule typically gives counties the option of changing forms of government. Counties are able to abandon the traditional commission system without central executive leadership in favor of either the county administrator or county executive forms. It gives localities the ability to change the method of election and the size of their

Table 2.1
States Ranked by Degree of Local Discretionary Authority, 1980

	A. Composite (all types of local units)	B. Cities Only	C. Counties Only	Degree of State Dominance of Fiscal Partnership*
1	Oregon	Texas	Oregon	2
2	Maine	Maine	Alaska	2
3	North Carolina	Michigan	North Carolina	1
4	Connecticut	Connecticut	Pennsylvania	2
5	Alaska	North Carolina	Delaware	1
6	Maryland	Oregon	Arkansas	2
7	Pennsylvania	Maryland	South Carolina	2
8	Virginia	Missouri	Louisiana	2
9	Delaware	Virginia	Maryland	1
10	Louisiana	Illinois	Utah	1
11	Texas	Ohio	Kansas	2
12	Illinois	Oklahoma	Minnesota	2
13	Oklahoma	Alaska	Virginia	1
14	Kansas	Arizona	Florida	2
15	South Carolina	Kansas	Wisconsin	1
16	Michigan	Louisiana	Kentucky	2
17	Minnesota	California	California	2
18	California	Georgia	Montana	3
19	Missouri	Minnesota	Illinois	2
20	Utah	Pennsylvania	Maine	2
21	Arkansas	South Carolina	North Dakota	1
22	New Hampshire	Wisconsin	Hawaii	3
23	Wisconsin	Alabama	New Mexico	2
24	North Dakota	Nebraska	Indiana	2
25	Arizona	North Dakota	New York	2
26	Florida	Delaware	Wyoming	2
27	Ohio	New Hampshire	Oklahoma	3
28	Alabama	Utah	Michigan	1
29	Kentucky	Wyoming	Washington	1
30	Georgia	Florida	Iowa	2
31	Montana	Mississippi	New Jersey	3
32	Washington	Tennessee	Georgia	2
33	Wyoming	Washington	Nevada	2
34	Tennessee	Arkansas	Tennessee	2
35	New York	New Jersey	Mississippi	3
36	New Jersey	Kentucky	New Hampshire	3
37	Indiana	Colorado	Alabama	2
38	Rhode Island	Montana	Arizona	2
39	Vermont	Iowa	South Dakota	2
40	Hawaii	Indiana	West Virginia	1
41	Nebraska	Massachusetts	Nebraska	3
42	Colorado	Rhode Island	Ohio	2
43	Massachusetts	South Dakota	Texas	3
44	Iowa	New York	Idaho	2
45	Mississippi	Nevada	Colorado	1
46	Nevada	West Virginia	Vermont	2
47	South Dakota	Idaho	Missouri	3
48	New Mexico	Vermont	Massachusetts	1
49	West Virginia	New Mexico	—	1
50	Idaho	—	—	2

*Key:
   1—State dominant fiscal partner.
   2—State strong fiscal partner.
   3—State junior fiscal partner.
   Applies to states in column A.

Source: U.S. Advisory Commission (1981), Table 20, p. 59.

legislative board or commission. In addition, it allows counties in some cases to move away from the long ballot tradition of electing many county administrative officials and to fill them by appointment instead. Structural home rule is supposed to give counties the power to institute changes in order to improve their ability to deal with the increasing complexity of contemporary policy problems.

Functional home-rule provisions allow counties the discretion to provide a wide and changing number of services that are not mandated by the state, but are supported by a majority of the county's voters. Functional home rule also refers to flexibility in the development of alternative service delivery mechanisms in these optional as well as mandated functions. The alternatives include contracting out to the private sector, contracting with another local government to produce a service (intergovernmental service contracts), service agreements for the joint provision of a service with another local government, and intergovernmental service transfers. The flexibility to choose between these alternatives presumably permits counties to maximize the effectiveness and efficiency of their operations through better management of their resources and to take greater advantage of economies of scale.

Home-rule provisions in fiscal administration are designed to permit counties to control their own finances (sources of revenue and long-term debt limits) and to promote budgetary stability. This flexibility is presumably necessary in light of the increasing diversity of responsibilities demanded by citizens and mandated by state governments. These provisions allow local governments to diversify their sources of revenue. Traditionally, counties have relied heavily on property taxes and intergovernmental aid as their primary sources of revenue. However, counties have been moving away from a reliance on property taxes to other sources of revenue such as sales taxes, user fees, and local income taxes. According to a recent report, 31 states permit local governments to levy sales taxes, and over one-third of American counties receive this source of revenue (Todd, 1991, 23). As popular citizen revolts against burdensome property taxes have occurred, county governments, like other local governments, have become more interested in exploiting other revenue options. As Figure 2.2 indicates, while intergovernmental aid accounts for the largest portion of county revenue (34.7%), and property tax ranks second (26.9%), current charges and miscellaneous revenue (24.7%) also serve as primary sources.

Unfortunately, while the need for financial independence may be great, this area of home-rule authority has traditionally lagged behind the structural and functional areas. Many states retain fiscal control over their

Figure 2.2
Percentage Distribution of Total County Revenues, 1988–89 (total: $119.8 billion)

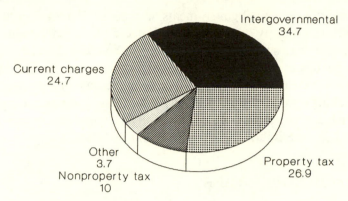

Source: U.S. Bureau of the Census.

county units with regard to the ability to raise revenue, acquire debt, and pass a budget. New Hampshire, for example, requires the representatives from each county in the House of Representatives to pass the annual county budget.

Home-rule authority, whether at the county or municipal level, is undoubtedly one of the more understudied areas of local government. This may, of course, be due to the often complex and unique character of home-rule provisions across the 50 states. What remains unanswered, however, is the impact of home-rule provisions on the operation of local government. It has been suggested, for instance, that a lack of home-rule authority may lead to greater reliance on special district governments, which often have independent taxing ability and may not be subject to the debt limitations placed on county units. This issue was studied in some limited research of Illinois county governments, which indicated that the lack of functional and fiscal autonomy can lead to increases in the need for such single-purpose units of government (Chicoine and Walzer, 1985). A great deal of additional research of this type must be done, however, before such a conclusion can be generalized to county governments around the nation.

While counties in most areas serve as the unit of local government between the municipal and state levels, several deviations from this model exist. In a number of urban metropolitan areas, the county government and one or more municipal governments have merged their structure and operation to form a consolidated city-county government (see Chapter 10). Some of the better-known examples of this type of government are

Indianapolis-Marion County, Indiana; Jacksonville-Duvall County, Florida; and New Orleans-Orleans Parish, Louisiana (the oldest consolidation dating back to 1805).

A number of municipal governments have obtained a legal status from their states that closely corresponds with traditional county status. Such "independent" cities perform the functions of both city and county government but operate completely independent of any county unit. This type of local government unit is found primarily in the state of Virginia, where upon reaching a population of 5,000 any incorporated community can seek state legislative approval for independent city designation. Other independent cities include Baltimore, Maryland, and St. Louis, Missouri.

FORMS OF GOVERNMENT

While a wide variety of structural arrangements exist for policy-making and implementation in American counties, there are three basic forms: commission, county administrator, and county executive. The commission form of county government historically has been the most common. It is primarily because of home-rule and local government reform movements that counties have begun to adopt alternative forms.

The commission or plural executive form is commonly characterized by a fusion of legislative and executive authority in an elected county commission or board of supervisors. In many cases, the degree of overlap between the commission's legislative and executive roles varies depending on the number of elected executive officials or row officers sharing the executive role. Generally, these row officers include county clerk, coroner, sheriff, treasurer, attorney or solicitor, and tax assessor. The commission, which is usually made up of three or five members (but can be larger), adopts a county budget, passes laws and ordinances, appoints advisory boards and commissions, and may appoint (or serve as) department heads of some executive departments.

The commission form presents several obstacles for the effective management of counties, especially urban ones. The lack of a strong unified position with executive responsibility for the operations of the entire county can create tremendous fragmentation of the system, promoting chaos, inefficiency, and little centralized public accountability. Further, the individual row officers often lack professionalism. This is not surprising given that these executive officials typically operate in a political climate with a low degree of public awareness or scrutiny and may be reelected routinely with little or no serious competition. Due to these and other inherent problems associated with this form, the *Model County Charter* stresses the need for a single appointed official (or elected executive) to administer the county with a representative policy-making council or board responsible for the legislative function.

The county administrator form is virtually a carbon copy of the city manager plan for American municipalities. Voters elect a legislative body to make policy and hire an appointed executive, responsible to the legislature, to carry out policies and oversee the day-to-day administration of the executive departments. However, the county government tradition of electing numerous executive officers has been very strong. As a result, there are few counties that give their appointed professional executive the powers commensurate with those of an American city manager. There appear to be three subtypes within this form of county government. In the "pure" council-manager version, the county manager exercises broad executive power, including setting the legislative agenda, developing the county budget, appointing department heads, and hiring county staff. The chief administrative officer (CAO) version of this form substitutes an appointed executive with fewer formal powers. He or she may have authority to coordinate and supervise the implementation of policies within the county departments, but does not have the power to appoint or fire department heads. The weakest version involves the hiring of a county administrative assistant. This person is a professional public administrator, but has few if any formal powers. He or she primarily performs tasks and gives advice at the request of the council or board.

The county executive form is analogous to the strong mayor plan for municipalities. There is a separation of powers with an executive separately elected at large from the legislature. County executives typically have the power to set the budgetary and legislative agendas for the council, appoint and remove department heads, veto acts of the legislature, and oversee the operations of the executive departments. A version of this form can include the hiring of a professional administrator to assist the county executive.

In order to obtain information on the use of various forms of county government, the International City Management Association (ICMA) conducted a "County Form of Government" survey in 1988. Questionnaires were sent to county clerks in all of America's 3,042 counties. Officials were given two attempts to respond. Completed surveys were obtained from 1,295 jurisdictions (42.5 percent). Counties in the highest population categories are slightly overrepresented as they were somewhat more likely to respond. Overall, a plurality of jurisdictions (39.7 percent) indicated that they use the commission form, 38.2 percent use the county administrator form, and 22.1 percent use the county executive form

(DeSantis, 1989). Although the commission governments are probably slightly underrepresented, these data indicate a substantial shift away from the traditional county structure. In this respect, the results are like those reported in a NACo study (Jeffery, Salant, and Boroshok, 1989).

Predictably, the distribution of county forms of government varies substantially by population size, geographic region, and metropolitan status. The commission form is least likely to be found in counties with the largest populations and most likely in the smallest jurisdictions. The proportion of commission counties increases substantially in communities with fewer than 25,000 people. County administrator forms are the most likely in counties with mid-sized to large populations, although their usage appears to be growing in all population categories. County executive governments tend to increase in usage with population size. The highest concentration of this system is in jurisdictions with over 250,000 residents.

On a geographic basis, commission governments are most likely in the Plains and Mountain states and least likely in the South and Pacific Coast. County administrator forms are the most likely in the South Atlantic, Mid-Atlantic, and Pacific Coast states and least likely in the West North Central, East South Central, and West South Central regions. The county executive form appears to be most likely in the East South Central and West South Central areas and least likely in the Pacific Coast, Mountain, and South Atlantic regions.

Some of the regional patterns are influenced, in part, by concentrations of particular forms in one or more states. For example, in North Carolina and South Carolina almost all of the counties operate with a version of the county administrator plan. Likewise, nearly all of the counties in Arkansas, Kentucky, and Tennessee operate under the county executive plan.

With respect to the metropolitan status of counties, commission systems are most likely in the nonmetropolitan "independent" counties. While county administrator forms are most likely in suburban counties, county executive governments are most prevalent in counties with a central city.

Surprisingly, there are few research projects evaluating the policy consequences of adopting different county forms of government. The indictments of the commission system and presumed strengths of the county administrator and county executive forms are well articulated in the literature and popular commentary. However, there remains little systematic (as opposed to anecdotal) evidence to support these assessments.

In contrast, the impact of municipal structures has been examined from a variety of different perspectives for more than two decades. In their classic 1967 study, Robert Lineberry and Edmund Fowler found that reformed cities tended to tax less and spend less than unreformed cities (p. 716). The latter, however, were found to be the most responsive to the socioeconomic characteristics of different constituencies. Since that seminal work, numerous researchers have employed a number of designs (cross-sectional, longitudinal, and panel studies) and measures to reinvestigate the impact of structure upon policy outputs. The resulting body of literature has not uniformly supported the conclusions of Lineberry and Fowler. At the very least, this suggests we should exercise caution in making unequivocal statements about the linkage between forms of local government and their presumed consequences.

Mark Schneider and Kee Ok Park have recently attempted to research this issue for counties (1989). Using data from 1977, they examined the per capita expenditures (total, developmental, and redistributive) and number of functions performed (total, developmental, and redistributive) of 162 counties located in 50 of the largest Metropolitan Statistical Areas (MSAs). After controlling for the effect of region and population size, Schneider and Park discovered that county executive jurisdictions spent the most and performed the most functions in all three categories. County administrator jurisdictions were consistently second in spending and functions and commission forms were consistently last. The structural differences were more dramatic for per capita expenditures than for number of functions performed. In fact, county executive governments spent more than twice the per capita expenditures of commission systems.

Recent research by the authors of this chapter, which updates the Schneider and Park investigation with 1988 financial data, reveals a somewhat different trend with county administrator jurisdictions spending the greatest amount per capita and county executive jurisdictions close behind. Both of these reformed types did spend significantly more than unreformed commission types, however (DeSantis and Renner, 1992a). This research raises the classic "chicken or egg" question: Is it different structural arrangements that actually lead to greater expenditures, or is it that counties whose service roles are increasing dramatically are the most likely to change forms of government to supposedly help them manage their growth?

ELECTION SYSTEMS

County election systems have historically been different from those of American municipalities. In particular, the former were less likely than the latter to experience Progressive Era reform. While a majority of cities adopted at-large and nonpartisan elections, counties generally maintained district and partisan elections. District elections require the subdivision of the county into wards or districts and the election of one (singlemember districts) or more (multimember districts) representatives from each of these smaller geographic units. District elections, which can provide better representation to minority groups in a county, suffer from the often-contentious problem of redrawing district boundaries—a process often leading to charges of gerrymandering. The U.S. Supreme Court, in *Avery v. Midland County*, mandated that general-purpose local governments must abide by the "one man-one vote" principle in the design of council districts. At-large elections, on the other hand, allow candidates for county council to run countywide campaigns and be elected by all geographic areas of the jurisdiction.

The revised edition of the *Model County Charter* provides several alternatives for the conduct of county elections. Individual counties may choose an at-large model, at-large elections with district residency requirements, single-member districts, a mixed district and at-large system, and a proportional representation system.

Proportional and semiproportional representation systems, such as cumulative voting, limited voting, and the single-transferable vote, are alternative voting systems that have been experimented with on the local level but remain infrequently used in modern electoral politics (Zimmerman, 1990). Limited voting, employed in a number of Connecticut towns and Pennsylvania counties, is a process in which citizens are allowed to vote for a specific number of candidates fewer than the number of candidates to be elected to the council (typically three votes if five members are to be elected). This makes it impossible for a party or group with the largest number of votes to win a disproportionate share of seats.

Cumulative voting allows each citizen to cast a specified number of votes (usually three) that can be apportioned as follows: three votes to one candidate, one vote to each of three candidates, two votes to one candidate and one to another candidate, or one and a half votes to each of two candidates. Although somewhat more complicated, this system can enhance minority representation because it allows smaller groups of voters to cast all their votes for the candidate of their choice, while the majority group or party may split behind and elect several of its candidates.

Proportional voting systems with the single transferable vote are designed to ensure that each party or group will receive the number of seats on any council in direct proportion to its voting strength. In this system, voters indicate a gradation of preferences for candidates on the ballot. This system can cost a great deal more to administer because of the complicated tallying of votes that must follow the actual election.

While a number of traditional and alternative election systems exist, the *Model County Charter* places great emphasis on the notion that local needs dictate the most acceptable method of elections. However, long-standing controversy and a large body of case law has surrounded the types of election systems used in American cities and counties.

When the U.S. Congress extended the Voting Rights Act in 1982, it amended Section 2 to strike down election systems that had racially discriminatory effects, regardless of intent. The Supreme Court had previously held, in *Mobile v. Bolden*, that intent was a necessary condition to challenge successfully an election system or procedure. This shift in national policy increased the number of lawsuits alleging racially discriminatory consequences in at-large elections. Although both cities and counties have been subject to these challenges, they have had a disproportionate impact upon municipalities since they were the most likely to use at-large procedures. Recent research by ICMA indicates that there was about a seven percentage point drop in the proportion of cities using at-large elections between 1981 and 1988 (Renner, 1988). Despite the decline, the survey of 4,631 municipalities indicated that a solid majority (60.4 percent) still used at-large elections. District elections were reported in only 12.8 percent of the cities and "mixed" systems were reported in 26.8 percent.

This is in stark contrast to the latest ICMA "County Form of Government" survey (1988), which indicates that a plurality of counties (45.5 percent) use district elections compared to 30.1 percent for "mixed" systems and only 24.4 percent for at-large systems. Predictably, the distribution of election system types varied by county population size, region, and metropolitan status. At-large elections were most likely in the very smallest counties, in the Mid-Atlantic and Mountain states, and in jurisdictions outside MSAs (DeSantis, 1989).

The differences between American cities and counties are even more dramatic in the proportions with partisan or nonpartisan elections. According to the most recent national survey, cities use nonpartisan over partisan systems by a margin of 72.6 to 27.4 percent. Counties, on the other hand, use partisan over nonpartisan elections by an even greater margin of 82.4 to 17.6 percent. Unlike municipalities, there were few major differences in the ratio of partisan to nonpartisan systems by a county's population size, region, or metropolitan status. The only exception was among those jurisdictions in the Pacific Coast states that reported having a narrow majority of nonpartisan systems.

As with county forms of government, there are very few research projects that have examined the policy or representational consequences of American county election systems. A recent work by the authors examined the impact of election systems (at-large, district, and mixed) upon minority and gender representation in American county legislatures (DeSantis and Renner, 1992b). They concluded that district elections produce the most equitable minority representation, at-large elections produced the least equitable results, and mixed systems were, predictably, between the two extremes. Female representation, however, was not found to vary significantly by type of county election system. Much more research, however, is necessary to determine whether and how differences in county election procedures matter.

SUMMARY

Counties have become a more important feature of the American federalist system. Citizens and other levels of government alike have called on counties to provide a more diverse array of services. With these increasing responsibilities, states have recognized the need to allow for greater degrees of discretionary authority. While many institutional and operational reforms came much more slowly for counties, they have undoubtedly brought them a long way from the "dark continent." Counties should continue to increase their service delivery role over the next decade, especially in areas like environmental protection and land-use planning, which call for more regional approaches. At the same time, however, counties will continue to be called on to provide the traditional services that have long been their domain. Thus, the continued reform and innovation of county government is essential for keeping the organization and management capacities in line with the demands of the next century.

Chapter 3

Legislatures and Legislating in County Government

Alvin D. Sokolow

Almost 30 years ago I wrote a dissertation on the legislative politics of two small Illinois counties. The two county boards of supervisors at that time practiced a brand of limited government. While differing in collegial interaction and informal rules, both boards operated primarily as administrators rather than policymakers. Decisions about road and bridge improvements dominated their policy agendas and were the major sources of intraboard conflict and citizen interest. All board members were white males and most were farmers. Elected as Democrats and Republicans, they conducted a portion of their business according to party lines (Sokolow, 1964).

So much has happened to county government since that time that it hardly seems useful today to try to draw lessons from the long-ago experiences of two governing boards in the rural Midwest. County policy agendas are much more expansive now, as the result of ever-increasing state and federal mandates, enlarged citizen appetites for county services, and the challenges of population and land use change in many parts of the nation. As compared to past times also, county boards have access to more information and expertise, both inside and outside their governments, to help make decisions and administer programs.

We cannot say, however, that such developments have largely displaced the traditional features of county board politics as I described them three decades ago. Examining the blend of old and new, this chapter is a sketch of the legislative organization and performance today of county governments. It concentrates on the dual roles of county governing boards as administrators and policymakers. Performance certainly is affected by formal organization—by aspects of representation, membership, and leadership. The starting point of this analysis is to compare the organizational features of county boards with those of city councils.

Not as well known as city councils, county boards are seldom studied as collegial institutions with representative, administrative, and policymaking functions.[1] This chapter draws selectively from a wide variety of case study and other research material, much of it specific to individual states. We rely as well on the published and unpublished findings of a recent study of county governments in four small communities in Illinois and California. As part of the Rural Capacity Project, which also included eight small municipal governments in the two states, legislative behavior in the four sample counties was studied largely through extensive field research in the early and mid-1980s. The four county governments all served similarly sized communities in the 11,000–21,000 population (1980) range, but the two California governments were substantially larger organizations—in service responsibilities, budgets, and employees—than the two Illinois governments.[2]

COUNTY-CITY DIFFERENCES IN ORGANIZATION

Nationwide, county governing boards go by 17 different formal titles. "Commissioners" and "supervisors" head the list, but there are also "councils," "county courts," "freeholders," and assorted other state-by-state variations (T. Salant, 1991).

These titles and the basic forms of county legislatures go back to the creation of county government by individual states, usually in their first constitutions. In organization most boards today are derivatives of two major forms—the "supervisor" or "township" form and the "commission" type (Duncombe, 1977, 51–56; Snider, 1957, 121–123; Jeffery, Salant, and Boroshok, 1989). Originating in New York and New Jersey and spreading primarily to the Midwest, the former type called for relatively large boards based on the representation of town or township governments.[3] More common nationwide are versions of the commission form, typically with three- or five-member boards, which originated in Pennsylvania. A primarily southern version of the commission arrangement attaches judicial titles ("judge," "justices of the peace," etc.) to separately elected board chairmen or individual commissioners, but with judicial functions no longer operative in most cases.

A more distinctive picture of county board organization emerges in a comparison with municipal councils, the other major type of legislative

Table 3.1
Organizational Characteristics of County Boards and Municipal Councils

	County Boards	Municipal Councils
	Data for All Governments	
Total governments nationwide	3,042	19,200
Total board/council members	17,014	106,791
Average number of members per board/council	5.6	5.6
% members elected by district	72.1	19.6
Average number of other (nonlegislative) elected officials per government	9.5	1.4
ICMA-recognized management positions, 1988		
Council-manager	100	2,735
General management	184	932
Total	284	3,667
% of all governments	9.4	19.0
	Sample Data	
% of boards/councils using partisan elections	82.4	27.4
% of presiding officers independently elected	22.0	77.7

Sources: 1987 Census of Governments Vol 1, No 2, *Popularly Elected Officials*,
Tables 8 and 10; *The Municipal Yearbook, 1989*, 25–32, 64; *The Municipal
Yearbook, 1988*, 61.

body in general-purpose local government. As Table 3.1 indicates, county
and city legislatures throughout the nation are alike in average size—5.6
members for each. But there are striking contrasts in several other aspects
of formal structure.

Representation. Election from districts is the prevailing form of representation for county boards, while at-large arrangements dominate city
councils. Almost three-quarters of all county board members nationwide
represent districts, as compared to only one-fifth of city council members.

Other elected officials. The well-known county practice of electing
numerous administrative officers is put into sharp relief by the comparison
in Table 3.1—an average of 9.5 nonlegislative elected officials for county
governments and only 1.4 for municipalities.

Appointed administrators. This comparison points out the relatively
limited employment of chief administrative officers by county boards.
Table 3.1 notes that less than 10 percent of all county governments have
"professional management" positions—including managers—recognized
by the International City Management Association, as compared to 19

percent for municipalities. In fact, about 26 percent of all county governments employ CAOs of one type or another (Jeffery, Salant, and Boroshok, 1989), but most such positions lack the authority typically granted strong managers, especially in the areas of personnel and policy formulation. The absence of appointed CAOs of any type or separately elected executives like city mayors in 60 percent of all counties means that most county legislative bodies have direct administrative responsibilities.

Partisanship. Partisan elections are the norm for county boards, while the great majority of municipal councils are elected on a nonpartisan basis. Among all regions, nonpartisan county elections dominate only in the Pacific Coast region. Both national and local political parties are represented in county board elections.

Board leadership. Most county boards select presiding officers from their own ranks. Board members usually rotate in and out of the chairmanship for one- or two-year terms. In contrast, the majority of mayors who preside over municipal councils are separately elected by the voters. County boards thus take on a more collegial character than municipal councils, with their chairperson lacking the independent status enjoyed by most city mayors.

As compared to city councils, then, county boards are relatively district-oriented, partisan, and collegial. They share power with other elected officials and lack the assistance of strong central administrators. How these formal conditions influence the everyday work of county legislatures is a central theme of the following sections.

GOVERNING BOARD ROLES: THE EMPHASIS ON ADMINISTRATION

As local legislatures, both county boards and city councils carry out a mix of activities. They represent constituents, deliberate and make policy, administer bureaucracies, and resolve public disputes (Svara, 1990, 123). To this list can be added a fifth legislative function grown more prominent in recent years: the conduct of intergovernmental relations.

It is the administrative role that dominates the activity of many county boards, more so than city councils.[4] In large part this is due to the limited employment of professional chief administrators in county government, imposing on legislators the necessity for immersing themselves in the management of their governments (Sokolow, 1984). But the emphasis on administration is also rooted in some long-standing ideas about the obligations of elected officeholders in county government that obscure the distinction between policy and administration. Many county legislators actually prefer to deal with nuts-and-bolts issues rather than with more abstract policy questions. Especially in less populated communities, there is little risk in serving constituents by concentrating on the familiar and immediate tasks of government. "Visible responses such as this are the stuff that get commissioners reelected," according to one account of Minnesota county government, describing how county board committees conduct personal inspections of road repairs and snowplow operations (Lease, 1977, 343).

Finding hard evidence about the administrative work of county legislators is not difficult. We have one measure in the formal proceedings of the four county boards in California and Illinois studied as part of the Rural Capacity Project. Table 3.2 indicates how each board, in a regular meeting in 1983 or 1984, allocated the time spent in discussing and acting on various topics. Administrative issues, as compared to policy and regulatory items, monopolized each board's agenda—more than 80 percent of total meeting time for the Illinois counties and somewhat less for the California jurisdictions. The administrative matters reviewed by the boards included bill payments, other fiscal details, numerous reports by department heads, contracts, purchase decisions, and personnel decisions. Because of community growth and the larger sizes and greater activity of their governments, the California boards devoted substantial portions (but still less than the time given to administrative items) of their sessions to policy and regulatory issues, including land use, planning, and water development matters.[5]

Board members of course spend time on county business outside of formal meetings. While it is conceivable they could be working on policy issues at these times—gathering policy-relevant information, for example—interviews with the California and Illinois legislators indicated that their other activities largely involved constituency contacts, consultations with department heads and other county staff, and meetings of board oversight committees. The California legislators also were active in intergovernmental matters, sitting as members of multicounty agencies, talking to a variety of state government departments, and attending frequent meetings of the statewide association of county supervisors.

"Less than full-time, but more than part-time" is how county board members frequently describe their schedules. The implication is that because of the administrative demands of board work, they put more time into their public positions than is ordinarily expected of citizen-officeholders in local government. In a mid-1980s study of local officials in nonmetropolitan areas of Ohio (Hines and Napier, 1985), county commissioners reported that they worked an average of 33.8 hours a week on public business, more time than city mayors (19.7) and township trustees (15.7).

Table 3.2
Time Devoted to Administrative and Other Topics at Meetings of Four County Boards

	Illinois Counties	
	CUMBERLAND (6/14/83) Total meeting time: 1 hour, 29 min*	DOUGLAS (1/17/84) Total meeting time: 2 hours, 30 min
Administrative items		
Minutes, finance	27 minutes	40 minutes
Contracts, agreements, bids	24	43
Personnel	19	0
Other reports	8	25
Other	5	15
Total (% of total time)	83 (93%)	123 (82%)
Regulatory items		
Subdivisions, zoning	6 (7%)	15 (10%)
Policy items		
Jail site selection	0	12 (8%)

	California Counties	
	GLENN (11/1/83) Total meeting time: 5 hours, 21 mins	AMADOR (5/24/83) Total meeting time: 3 hours, 57 min
Administrative items		
Minutes, finance	12 minutes	28 minutes
Contracts, bids	131	22
Personnel**	24	34
Other reports	13	68
Other	0	12
Total (% of total time)	180 (56%)	164 (69%)
Regulatory items--permits, land use hearings, etc.	77 (24%)	47 (20%)
Citizen complaints	0	7 (3%)
Policy items--water supply, economic development, planning	65 (20%)	19 (8%)

* Total meeting time does not include recesses, other pauses.
** Includes executive sessions devoted to personnel and other items.
Source: Field observations of county board meetings, Rural Capacity Project.

Likewise, county board members in our two-state study generally reported longer work weeks than municipal council members. The California county legislators were virtually full-time officials, with several reporting 40-hour or more workweeks, although their annual compensation fell below the standards of middle-income earners in their communities (Sokolow, 1987).

The administrative work of most county boards probably is less concentrated on the direct supervision of service delivery than on the oversight of programs. While legislators typically get involved in personnel decisions, budget preparation, and purchasing, they intervene much less frequently in the internal management of departments, as suggested by patterns in our four California and Illinois counties (Sokolow, 1986). One reason is the control of sizable portions of county bureaucracies by separately elected administrators, including sheriffs, county clerks, and assessors. But even for the programs they directly control through the appointment of department heads—such as public works and social services—governing boards over the years have pulled back from direct involvement in departmental administration. This trend is a response to the growing complexity of individual county government programs and the increasing professionalism of department-level administration (Koehler, 1983, 30).

Administrative oversight by county boards in our four counties was largely accomplished through standing committees (individual member assignments in one county), as in county governments elsewhere (Wenum, 1991; B. Davis, 1991). Organized into as many as 25 committees for a seven-member board (the largest in the four-county sample), board members closely monitored developments in individual departments and programs. Decision-making authority was not delegated to committees or individual members; they were not able in unilaterial fashion to hire employees, spend funds, or otherwise commit their county governments. Rather, the committees were agents of their larger boards, information-gatherers and liaisons to individual programs. Department heads and other program supervisors brought specific problems to the committees, and used them as sounding boards for new ideas (Sokolow, 1986).

The administrative emphasis is usually traced to the rural roots of county government, to a simpler past when county governments had fewer and primarily courthouse functions mandated by the state (Duncombe, 1977, ix; Snider, 1957, 131–134). Yet it lingers on, even as policy concerns have proliferated and counties have become more active, notably in suburban and urban areas. Legislators in both large and small counties, with or without professional administrators, like to keep their hands on some management tasks, anecdotal evidence suggests. Hillsborough County (Tampa), Florida, with a population of 776,000 in 1986, had employed chief administrators for almost two decades. But individual commissioners continued to involve themselves in specific service delivery matters, such as asking public works crews to attend to particular projects. The professionalization of the bureaucracy had not destroyed the belief in direct and personal service to constituents (Gurwitt, 1989).

More systematic research supports the general point. The study of Georgia and Florida county board members by Marando and Thomas

(1977, 91) in the late 1970s showed little relationship between commissioners' perceived administrative-legislative job activities and the size and urbanization of counties. Also lacking was a strong relationship with professional administration. Board members in counties with appointed administrators were only slightly less likely to emphasize administrative duties in their own jobs.

POLICY INNOVATION

Regardless of how comfortable the administrative emphasis may be, county boards in many parts of the nation today cannot avoid a more active policy role. County governments have taken on additional programs in recent years and their constituents have become more demanding. Consequently, their legislatures, particularly in suburban and urbanizing areas, have had to cope with numerous service delivery and population growth issues (Marando and Thomas, 1977, 25; Koehler, 1983; Murphy and Rehfuss, 1976, 144–145; Gurwitt, 1991).

Administration and policy-making are not necessarily mutually exclusive activities. And while the proportions of the two vary from one government to another, county board members may be less motivated in their actions by the administration-policy dichotomy than by the relative appeal of different issues. This is one implication of the Marando-Thomas study (1977, 83–86), which found that Georgia and Florida commissioners in the 1970s were more active—as both administrators and policy deliberators—in certain program areas than in others. In particular, road programs and financing attracted much involvement, while law enforcement and welfare stimulated less activity. County legislators everywhere prefer to tackle programs in which they have some local control and which are popular with constituents, than those that are complicated by state and federal mandates (Giles, et al., 1980; Giventer and Neeley, 1984).

How then do county boards perform as policymakers? Based on the evidence of past decades, they have a reputation for cautious and conservative behavior when approached with new or long-term problems. Low taxing and spending ideologies conventionally have been major obstacles to change. What policy innovation took place usually originated outside county government and was accepted only reluctantly by county boards. Examples abound from the post-World War II period—county boards in the suburban Philadelphia area responding to the policy initiatives of private interest groups (Gilbert, 1967, 214–215); plans for a county airport in upstate New York instigated by Chamber of Commerce leaders (Mann and Stout, 1963); a similar story of the effort to organize a community college in another New

York state county (Scholl, 1963); and the opposition of the board governing the county surrounding Syracuse, New York, to new functions promoted by state and city officials (Martin, et al., 1965, 324).

Perhaps this is an unfair and overly simplistic characterization, one that is faulted by dated patterns. The evidence in any event is sketchy, since county board behavior is not studied systematically nor on a broadly generalizable basis. But more recent case studies present some significant illustrations of board-initiated policy development and suggest the conditions leading to such innovation. Perceived environmental threats and the costs of growth in small or medium-sized communities, for example, seem to explain why boards in a number of Midwestern counties in the 1970s established stricter zoning and other ordinances to protect farmland (Barrows and Libby, 1981), and why the Santa Barbara County (California) Board of Supervisors in the 1980s moved aggressively to regulate the onshore aspects of offshore oil projects (Lima and Woolley, 1990).

Examples of both policy leadership and resistance to innovation on the part of county boards are found in the Rural Capacity study. Legislators in the two California counties had ambitious policy agendas in the early 1980s, taking the lead on such projects as regional water development, county hospital reorganization, and justice court consolidation. The California boards also were heavily involved in land use planning and regulatory actions, devoting substantial board and staff time to the review of development proposals.

The two Illinois county boards operated in a much more narrow context. Their few actions that could possibly qualify as "policy innovation" in the early 1980s included the state-required enlargement of one jail, the purchase of a private building to accommodate crowded courthouse offices, and the creation of a part-time public defender's position. Illustrating the resistance to new spending, legislators in one county initially refused to help a village government fund a public ambulance service. The village had taken over the operation after it was abandoned by local funeral homes, and then approached the county board to support service to areas outside the village limits. Concerned about higher taxes on farmland and unwilling to tap their general fund, the county legislators agreed to participate in the program only after others suggested a special property tax levy based primarily on nonfarm property.

DECISION PATTERNS: THE ROLE OF CONFLICT

Whether innovative or not, the actions of county boards are substantially influenced by their organizational features. District representation, partisan office, and the presence of numerous other elected officials, for example, are likely sources of conflict among board members. Adding further to the potential for conflict is the diversity and geographical diffusion of the constituencies served by county governments—combining rural, suburban, and urban populations in many cases (Marando and Thomas, 1977, 40). Municipal governments serve more homogeneous and concentrated communities by comparison.

Save for one study that implies that county commissioners in Ohio experience relatively high levels of conflict because they perceive more job stress than other local officials (Hines and Napier, 1985), there is no evidence that county boards are more or less conflictual than city councils. High degrees of board unanimity are reported for Georgia and Florida counties, based on the perceptions of board members (Marando and Thomas, 1977, 99), but they are elected at large in both states. It is questionable that legislative conflict can be measured in a meaningful way by mail surveys or according to formal roll calls.[6] As in other legislative bodies, collegial pressures and the desire to avoid personal animosities tend to suppress overt signs of conflict in the work of county boards.

Some conflict-related patterns are apparent in the legislative work of county boards, such as the following effects of the organizational features previously identified.

Rural-urban splits. The separate representation of county and town districts leads to a basic division on many boards, especially where a single population center (typically the county seat) is the dominant economic and social influence in the county. Mere geography by itself is not the cause of the division. It needs to be accompanied by other differences between county and town residents and their legislative representatives, in such areas as ideology, expectations about the appropriate functions of county government, and perceptions regarding the fair distribution of taxes and services. Thus rural residents of Missoula (Montana) in the 1980s resented the imposition of land use controls by an urban-controlled board (Manning, 1988). Also in the 1980s, rural commissioners in Greenville County (South Carolina) successfully opposed the plan for a county-city colosseum on the grounds that downtown interests would be subsidized by county taxpayers (Ehrenhalt, 1991, 95–96).

Allocational politics. District representation also has the potential for stimulating intraboard competition for geographically divisible benefits. Most often this means competition among districts for road and bridge improvements, traditionally the most visible and valuable of all county government services because of their importance to farm families and other rural residents. At more than $8 billion annually, highway maintenance and construction is now the third largest expenditure for counties nationwide, exceeded only by public welfare and education spending. Some county governments in recent years have given professional engineers the discretion to allocate road and bridge funds. But in many counties, legislators still tenaciously hang on to the transportation purse strings. Logrolling is the traditional practice—the localization of road construction and maintenance decisions, permitting each board member to control crews and projects in his or her district. Recent accounts suggest that this is still the prevailing pattern among rural counties in Texas (Mladenka and Hill, 1989, 263), Mississippi (Giles et al., 1980), and Oklahoma (Hanson, 1965).

Partisanship. The reformist drive to remove political party labels from local elections, so successful in municipal government in the early part of the century, made less progress in county government. Perhaps because counties generally are the organizational base for political parties in the United States and county governments operate the nation's election machinery, few states established nonpartisan elections for county offices (Snider, 1957, 280; Duncombe, 1977, 69–70). Electoral partisanship may have greater implications for the selection of county board leaders than for the bulk of policy and administrative actions taken. It is taken for granted that the majority party on a board will want to select one of its own as chairperson, who in turn will favor party colleagues in the appointment of committee chairperson and members. Not uncommonly, however, party discipline can fail for factional or personal reasons, and bipartisan coalitions can control the organization of a board for a short period. Partisan elections of board members in the two Illinois counties included in the Rural Capacity project had little impact on board actions in the early 1980s, with one major exception. Anticipating the election of the first Democrat in many years as sheriff, the Republican-controlled board in one county shortly before the election withdrew the traditional offer of free living quarters for the office.

Power-sharing. County boards have an ambiguous relationship with their sheriffs, county clerks, treasurers, and other independently elected administrators. On the one hand, the "row" officers, frequently backed by strong countywide constituencies, command more political respect than appointed department heads. Depending on the state, many also have constitutional or statutory independence, making it difficult if not impossible for boards to deny their budget and other requests. On the other hand, conflict is inevitable when the boards try to legislate policy for all parts of their county governments. Personnel policies apparently are the major source of board-officer tension, according to examples from Illinois

(Wilson and Elder, 1987), Michigan (B. Davis, 1991), Montana (Manning, 1988), and Georgia and Florida (Marando and Thomas, 1977, 34). In such cases efforts by county boards to standardize employee benefits and other personnel practices clash with the desire of row officers to keep control over their staffs. Whatever the issue, the legislative maneuverability of county boards is much constrained by the independence of elected administrators.

CONCLUSIONS: QUESTIONS ABOUT LEGISLATURES AND LEGISLATORS

County governing boards in many respects share the characteristics of other democratically elected legislative bodies in American government. They represent constituents, control public revenues and expenditures, make policy, and appoint and oversee bureaucrats. Peering behind these generic similarities, however, we see some distinctive features, especially as compared to city councils, the other major type of legislative body in general-purpose local government.

In organization and behavior, county boards are more district-oriented, partisan, and constrained by other elected officials than city councils. Also they are less dependent on—or dominated by—appointed professional administrators and elected executives. It is true that many county boards in recent years have become more active policy innovators and regulators, especially on matters of community growth and environmental protection. But most probably are still enthusiastic administrators and, for the majority of issues, only reluctant policy innovators.

To a degree these are lingering features of the rural and limited government origins of American counties. Population growth, suburbanization, state and federal mandates, and more demanding constituencies have pushed county governments in the direction of professionalization and policy activity without removing entirely the traditional elements of legislative behavior. They linger because the essential character of county government has never changed—its ambiguity in both purpose and representation. Counties still perform in a double and often contradictory capacity as both local governments and administrative arms of their states. And they continue to serve diverse constituencies, mixtures of rural-suburban-urban populations with often conflicting values and demands.

The implications of these patterns are not fully explored in this brief sketch of county legislative behavior nor in the sparse research literature on the subject. There remain questions about the limits of administrative involvement, board-staff relationships, and the extent and sources of policy innovation. What is the process, for example, by which boards give up administrative involvement in favor of stronger appointed administrators? What internal norms do they adopt and maintain as collegial problem-solving groups?

We can also ask about the people who hold legislative office in county government. Concentrating on the collective actions of boards, this summary ignores the personal dimensions of the institution—individual legislators as citizens, representatives, and political leaders. About 17,000 persons serve in such elected posts nationwide. Who are they? How do they differ from other American legislators in gender, race and ethnicity, occupation, and community background?[7] How have these characteristics changed over the years, and with what consequences for policy and leadership? What motivates citizens to seek county legislative office? What are their political career patterns? And how do they represent constituents and develop policy orientations?

It seems that we have just begun to understand the legislative process in county government. As important agents of local democracy throughout the nation, county governing boards and their members deserve as much attention as other legislative institutions in American government.

NOTES

1. Perhaps the most detailed examination of county board members published to date is the Marando and Thomas (1977) study of Georgia and Florida commissioners conducted in the 1970s. Dealing primarily with individual commissioners' perceptions of issues and policy responsibilities, as gathered through a questionnaire survey, this research only minimally looked at the collective actions of boards.

2. In the early 1980s the two California counties each had annual expenditures of more than $18 million and employed more than 350 persons, as compared to expenditures and workforces one-fourth to one-tenth as much for the Illinois jurisdictions. The Rural Capacity Project was supported by the Economic Research Service of the U.S. Department of Agriculture, under a cooperative agreement with the University of California, Davis, with the author as principal investigator. Published products of the research include Sokolow (1984, 1986, 1987).

3. The equal-population rulings of the federal courts in the 1960s had a strong impact on county boards. Applied to local legislatures after the initial attack on the apportionments of state legislatures, the constitutional requirement of periodic reapportionment according to population affected all district-based boards. But the changes were the greatest for supervisor form boards in such states as Illinois and Wisconsin, where board members had to abandon their dual

roles as both township and county officials (Wenum, 1991, 60; Crane and Hagensick, 1976, 33).

4. In municipal governments without professional administrators or strong mayors, councils are involved in administration to a greater extent than in other cities. Similar to county boards, councils in such weak mayor-council munici-palities make extensive use of oversight committees (Svara, 1990, 124).

5. With relatively extensive agendas, the two California boards held regular, day-long meetings once a week, as compared to the two- or three-hour sessions conducted by the Illinois boards only once a month.

6. Nonunanimous votes accounted for 2–10 percent of all formal roll calls recorded in 1982 by the four counties in the California-Illinois study.

7. For the first time in its 1987 report, the Census of Governments collected and published information on the gender and racial makeup of local governing boards. Females were 9.1 percent and nonwhites were 5.7 percent of all county board members in that year, both less than the comparable proportions for city councils (U.S. Bureau of the Census, 1990, Tables 20–21).

Chapter 4

County Capacity and Intergovernmental Relations

William L. Waugh, Jr. and Gregory Streib

As the demands upon county governments in the United States have increased, the historical debate concerning the fiscal, policy-making, and administrative capacities of county governments has been renewed. To some extent, the questions concerning county government capacities are similar to those concerning municipal government capacities. But there are important differences—not the least of which relates to the status of county governments as agents of state administration and the limited discretion afforded counties under most state constitutions and statutes.

County governments, more so than municipal, are still generally perceived as lacking the capacities necessary to address local needs and to design, implement, finance, and operate effective programs. Because counties have been perceived to be arms of state government, the capacity debate has generally focused on both the willingness and ability of state officials to address local concerns through county offices. Only recently the debate has focused on the willingness and ability of county officials to address those needs directly.

Assessing county capacity is made even more difficult by the tremendous diversity in government structures, differences in state-local relationships, and the broad range in levels of administrative and political skill among county officials. County governance ranges from state-of-the-art service delivery to the quite primitive. There are counties delivering the most demanding services very effectively, and there are counties operating literally out of the garages and checkbooks of elected officials with little regard for fiscal accountability. Given those circumstances, what, then, are the major concerns about county government capacity generally? Just how capable are county officials of identifying local needs and designing, implementing, financing, and managing programs to address those needs? And, have state officials shown a willingness to build county government capacities? Those are the issues to be addressed here.

CAPACITY ISSUES

In general terms, the literature has tended to focus on issues of fiscal, political or policy-making, and administrative or managerial capacity. The fiscal capacity literature has generally dealt with tax bases and tax efforts (see, e.g., U.S. ACIR, 1982) and/or creative fiscal approaches. At issue are the financial resources available to the community, government's willingness and ability to extract those resources (and even community willingness to comply), and the sophistication of the financial management techniques utilized.

The political capacity literature has tended to focus on local policy-making discretion (Zimmerman, 1981) and/or the adoption of structural reforms (Streib and Waugh, 1990, 1991a and c). To a lesser extent, attention has been paid to the aptitude demonstrated by local officials in the area of "policy management" or how well those officials translate community values into a set of policy priorities and effective programs to address local needs (Burgess, 1975; Ostrowski, White, and Cole, 1984). Leadership training for elected officials, in fact, has become a priority in a number of states (Klinger, 1991).

The administrative capacity literature has generally focused on the sophistication of management techniques, including the integration of new technologies such as microcomputers, and/or the levels of professionalization among government workers. Administrative and political capacities have also been related to the abilities of local officials to accomplish what they wish or need to do (Honadle, 1981; Gargan, 1981; Waugh and Hy, 1988; Streib and Waugh, 1991a), rather than viewing "capacity" as an abstract. At best, fiscal, political, and administrative capacities are difficult to measure and it has been noted that "excess capacity" is both possible and, as it can reflect ineffective and inefficient use of resources, undesirable.

On the whole, the capacity literature supports the conclusion that the differences among county governments are often stark. Certainly some jurisdictions have better tax bases than others—indeed, some have very small bases and such meager fiscal resources that intergovernmental transfers are the only means of delivering the traditional county services. There are counties in Georgia, for example, in which the county government itself is the largest employer and state payrolls represent the largest contributions to the local economy. Suggestion of some consolidation of the 159 Georgia counties is met with understandable fear in those small rural counties. Although state regulation of local finances is increasing, there are still small jurisdictions in which officials pay county employees in cash or from personal checking accounts with little or no record-keeping. But that fiscal casualness is changing rapidly. Indeed, because counties have been legally tied to state government, regulation of county finances is somewhat easier than regulation of municipal finances. Similarly, increased concern over the representativeness of county government is leading to structural and electoral reforms. In Georgia, for example, one such reform has been a movement away from the single-commissioner forms of county government. By contrast, home-rule provisions in states like Florida now give local law precedence over state law in many areas (Waugh, 1976). The measurement of county fiscal, political, and administrative capacity is difficult at best, but the analysis to follow will provide some information on how county officials view their own circumstances.

INTERGOVERNMENTAL RELATIONS AND CAPACITY-BUILDING

The expectation of significant capacity-building was a central theme in the arguments for county home rule and city-county consolidation legislation during the first half of this century, particularly in terms of expanded taxing authority and policy-making discretion helping county officials respond to local needs. The movement for home rule charters and consolidations stalled, however, when fiscal resources and technical assistance became available to county governments directly through federal agencies in the late 1960s and early 1970s. At that time the major impetus for reform switched from expanded county taxing and borrowing powers and, perhaps to a lesser extent, political discretion to increased political and administrative capacities to deal with the new opportunities and new demands. The advent of revenue-sharing and block grant programs in the 1970s encouraged local involvement in the allocation of federal and state funds for programs but required compliance with federal and state mandates for those programs (Jones and Doss, 1978; Sylvester, 1989; D. M. Stewart, 1991). The newly found fiscal resources meant a lessened interest in capacities for effective government. Also, the mandates required greater attention to fiscal accountability and compliance with narrow administrative regulations, rather than encouraging greater local autonomy.

However, as budget cuts lessened the transfer of federal fiscal resources to counties during the Reagan years and the roles of county governments expanded, concerns grew about the abilities of county officials to address constituent needs effectively and, particularly, about their abilities to finance needed programs (D. M. Stewart, 1991; Todd, 1991; and, especially, Parks, 1991). Indeed, Robert B. Hawkins, chair of the U.S. Advisory Commission on Intergovernmental Relations, expressed in 1990 that expanding the "policy structures" that will facilitate local governments being able to address their own problems is a critical task for federal and state officials (Hawkins, 1990; Klinger, 1991). Local exercise of policy discretion, too, is limited by the resource drain due to the unfunded demands placed on county and city governments by state and federal mandates (Streib and Waugh, 1991a).

The issue, then, is the extent to which capacity-building is taking place. From the literature on municipal government, one would assume that all local officials are developing better skills and more effectiveness at addressing local problems (see, e.g., Poister and Streib, 1989; Streib and Poister, 1989). However, it is dangerous to generalize from the municipal government literature to county government (Marando and Reeves, 1990). Joseph F. Zimmerman (1981, 1983) does provide some measures of local government political capacity based on the states' willingness to permit discretionary authority in the areas of finance, personnel, function, and structure. In general terms, Zimmerman found that municipalities have more discretionary authority than counties. But, as David R. Berman and Lawrence L. Martin (1988) suggest, it is not always certain to what extent local governments can and do take advantage of the flexibility. In examining Zimmerman's indexes of discretion, Berman and Martin did find that the flexibility afforded to county governments by their states is "highly related" to the date when the state constitution was written, as well as to levels of urbanization, income, and education of the residents. In short, the limitations on flexibility are likely tied to the age of the constitution, and the increases in flexibility are tied to the political pressures brought to bear by relatively affluent, educated populations in more urbanized areas.

In terms of administrative capacity, when William A. Jones and C. Bradley Doss (1978) examined local (including county) officials' perceptions of federal efforts at capacity-building in the 1970s, they found that county officials acknowledged the need for technical assistance. The needs identified by county officials were similar to those expressed by city officials and included assistance with planning (52 percent), training for local staff (32 percent), management (28 percent), and budget formulation (24 percent). Smaller percentages of county officials expressed the need for assistance with goal setting (16 percent) or with citizen groups (8 percent). The larger concerns were with administrative issues, rather than more political ones. The more telling statistics on the ranking of technical assistance sources, however, suggest that local officials perceived the best sources to be internal or local staffs (70 percent), substate planning bodies (40 percent), state agencies (38 percent), consultants (32 percent), and city or county associations (30 percent). Only a small percentage (14 percent) ranked federal agencies in the top three important sources of technical assistance. In terms of assistance with local administration, officials tended to prefer local agencies over state agencies, and very few looked to the federal government.

In terms of more specific needs, a study in 1989 (Waugh and Streib, 1989) indicated that county officials felt the major barriers to effective county governance were excessive state mandates, inadequate revenues, constitutional or statutory limitations in local discretionary authority, excessive federal mandates, lack of support from state agencies, and lack of support from state elected officials (in that order). Much less concern was expressed about the capacities of county offices to manage programs well or to represent local interests. Indeed, the county officials demonstrated a very high level of confidence in their own government's capacities to both make policy and manage programs, although the officials did indicate considerable concern about local abilities to finance programs and the willingness of state officials to assume some part of the fiscal burden.

In a related study (Streib and Waugh, 1991c) 80 percent of county administrators and 71 percent of elected county executives indicated that limits on local discretionary authority were major problems. In terms of administrative issues, other major concerns were the retention of quality employees, the high number of elected department heads, conflict between elected officials and administrators, frequent changes in political leadership, and inadequate management systems (in that order). Major impediments to professionalism at the county level included poor financial rewards, low prestige of public service employment, and lack of opportunities for management training (in that order).

STATE OF THE COUNTIES

The aforementioned studies and analyses indicate that fiscal, political, and administrative capacity-building has generally been slow in county government and that progress varies widely from state to state and from county to county. Certainly there are county governments that are as administratively professional and politically responsive as any other governments in the

United States. But, just as certainly, there are county governments that are neither administratively competent nor politically representative. Although it can be argued that the latter group is no longer typical, it may be the group that discourages the expansion of county responsibilities. The image of nonprofessional, nonresponsive, and even corrupt county government discourages confidence in county officials generally.

Counties continue to have a restricted role in the intergovernmental system, in most respects still acting as vehicles for state governance and lagging behind city governments in grants of political and fiscal authority. As a consequence, administrative capacity-building has also been very slow. Nonetheless, county officials feel they are quite capable of assuming a more active role in addressing local needs. The perspective of county officials is illustrated in the survey results that follow.

How county officials view the current intergovernmental system and their own capacities is shown in Tables 4.1 and 4.2. County officials' perceptions of changes in local government responsibilities and authority in the years 1984 to 1989 are shown in Table 4.3. All three tables are based on data collected in 1989 and 1990 from a national survey of county administrators, elected county executives, and county commission chairpersons. The response rate was 40 percent.

As Table 4.1 indicates, county officials showed some ambivalence about whether state government has been responsive to their needs. They were much less ambivalent about whether the state legislatures have been responsive, with fully three-fourths indicating they do not think that to be the case. By contrast, the county officials were more evenly divided, with 44 percent agreeing and 57 percent disagreeing that state administrative agencies are responsive to local needs. While the negative estimate of legislative responsiveness is considerably greater, both sets of responses clearly indicate grave concerns about the responsiveness of state officials. Earlier studies in fact have indicated that most county officials believe that state governments have been more responsive to urban counties than they have to rural counties (e.g., Waugh and Streib, 1990), and indicate that state legislatures are the least responsive institutions (e.g., Streib and Waugh, 1990). The major concern expressed has been the willingness of state officials to provide fiscal resources for local government. The data here indicate that 91 percent believe that state government had not done as much as it could to provide fiscal support. Those attitudes are undoubtedly reflected in the responses to the question of whether county officials trust state government, with 61 percent indicating that they do not (also see Waugh, 1988).

Table 4.1 also indicates that county officials do not believe that the federal government has been responsive to their needs either—85 percent

Table 4.1

County Officials' Perceptions of Intergovernmental Relations (in percentages, n = 733)

Statement	Strongly Agree	Agree	Disagree	Strongly Disagree
State government is responsive to the needs of local governments in your state	2	40	45	14
The state legislature is responsive to the needs of counties like yours	1	24	50	25
State administrative departments are responsive to the needs of counties like yours	1	43	46	11
State government has done as much as it can financially to support local government programs in your state	1	8	48	43
Your state government has assumed its proper fiscal obligations to maintain public services at the local level	3	22	45	31
County officials in your state distrust state government	14	47	36	3
The federal government is responsive to the needs of county government in your state	1	14	59	26
The federal government is better able than your state government to address the kinds of serious problems that you have in your county	3	13	47	36
The federal government should use its revenue resources to assist state and local governments in your state	41	45	11	4

Note: Percentages may not add up to 100 due to rounding.
Source: Adapted from Streib and Waugh (1990).

of the officials disagreed with the statement that the federal government is responsive to county needs, and 83 percent disagreed with the statement that the federal government is better able than state government to address serious local problems. Notwithstanding those views, 86 percent of the county officials still believed that the federal government should provide fiscal resources to local governments.

In terms of the perceptions of county government capacities, not surprisingly Table 4.2 indicates that county officials are confident of their own and their offices' abilities to handle new responsibilities well—82 percent disagreed with the idea that their local government was administratively incapable of exercising new powers or responsibilities well. Indeed, while some critics of increased local authority and responsibility have argued that special interest groups will interfere with the representation of local interests, 75 percent of the county officials disagreed. Indeed, 97 percent of the officials felt that they, rather than state officials, were better able to address local needs. Much less confidence, however, was expressed about the capacities of county governments to generate new fiscal resources—80 percent indicated that they had done as much as they could to fund local public services.

Table 4.3 offers a different view of the capacities of county governments. When asked whether the administrative responsibilities of their county governments had increased during the past five years, 96 percent indicated that had been the case. By contrast, only 46 percent indicated that the policy-making or home-rule powers of their governments had increased during that period of time. Both statistics suggest that the administrative responsibilities and, to a lesser extent, political discretion of county officials increased significantly during the 1980s. But only about one-fifth of the county officials reported increases in taxing and borrowing authority (21 and 20 percent, respectively).

The picture of county government reflected in the responses of the officials is fairly consistent. There is considerable interest among county officials in expanding responsibilities and authority and quite high levels of confidence in their abilities. At the same time, there is concern that the states and, perhaps to a lesser extent, the federal government are passing on administrative responsibilities (e.g., mandates) without either transferring adequate fiscal resources to pay for them or permitting county governments to expand their own authority to generate such resources. The concerns with the expansion (or lack thereof) of political authority are consistent with the view that state officials have been centralizing policy-making at their own level rather than permitting the kinds of decentralized policy-making that were frequently cited as goals of the Reagan administration's "new federalism" initiatives. The expression of distrust of state officials may also reflect the frustration brought on by increasing administrative and political demands and the lack of fiscal resources with which to respond.

Table 4.2
County Officials' Perceptions of Local Government Capacity (in percentages, n = 733)

Statement	Strongly Agree	Agree	Disagree	Strongly Disagree
Your local government is administratively incapable of utilizing properly any additional powers or responsibilities that may be transferred to it by state government	2	13	39	43
Strong local economic and political interests will prevent county officials in your state from exercising any additional powers or responsibilities well	3	22	53	22
Your local government has done all it can financially to support local public services	41	39	19	2
Local officials are better able than state officials to respond to local needs	55	42	3	0
The powers and authority of county governments in your state are adequate to meet local needs	3	27	46	24
Local discretion in your state should be increased through the granting of more home-rule powers	45	46	8	1
Local taxing authority should be increased in your state so that communities can respond to local needs	44	40	13	3
Local borrowing authority should be increased so that communities and counties can respond to local needs	19	45	31	5

Note: Percentages may not add up to 100 because of rounding.
Source: Adapted from Streib and Waugh (1990).

CONCLUSIONS

In terms of the current state of county-federal and county-state relations, the evidence is relatively clear. County officials want to be viewed as full partners in the intergovernmental system, provided with adequate re-

Table 4.3

Increased County Authority and Responsibility in Past Five Years (in percentages, n = 733)

Change	Administrative Responsibility	Policy Authority	Taxing Authority	Borrowing Authority
Increase	96	46	21	20
No Increase	4	54	79	80
Totals =	100	100	100	100

sources to comply with federal and state mandates, and "empowered" by expanded discretionary (i.e., home-rule) powers and resources, as well as provided with assistance in specific policy areas, such as judicial services, jails, transportation, growth management, and health and human services (D. M. Stewart, 1991; Todd, 1991). An improved state-local relationship is even more critical given the tendency toward greater state control (Todd, 1991) and the current level of distrust (Waugh, 1988; Waugh and Streib, 1990). In terms of the capacities of county governments and county officials to design, implement, manage, and maintain effective policies and programs to address constituent desires and needs, the evidence is less clear. Certainly, there are county governments with considerable capability and very sophisticated means. Just as certainly, there are county governments that lack the political, fiscal, and administrative wherewithal to govern effectively. There is every reason to believe, however, that the situation is improving. The speed of that improvement will likely be dependent upon both necessity, as authority and responsibilities increase, and resources. It should also be mentioned that the perceptions and attitudes of county, city, state, and federal officials, as well as the public at large, also are important aspects of capacity-building. The low levels of trust undoubtedly affect the willingness to provide support and cooperation and good working relationships may be crucial as officials at all levels grapple with the major policy problems of the day.

Chapter 5

County Services: The Emergence of Full-Service Government

J. Edwin Benton and Donald C. Menzel

When Andrew P. O'Rourke, Westchester (New York) County executive, was elected in 1981 he did not have to deal with an AIDS problem or a homeless problem. Moreover, as he puts it, "we were getting money hand over fist from Washington" (*City & State*, February 11, 1991: 3). That has all changed. Federal revenue-sharing has ended and federal categorical and block grant money is not as plentiful. Costly state mandates abound.

Like Westchester County, many counties throughout the nation find themselves facing new problems and sometimes old problems (like solid waste disposal) that require new or innovative solutions. In Pinellas County (Florida), for example, medical care for the homeless is a problem. Consequently, Pinellas County organized a mobile medical care team that travels from St. Petersburg to Clearwater treating the homeless at soup kitchens and emergency shelters. Using a mobile van equipped with medical supplies and staffed by a doctor, a nurse, a social worker, and a support person, the county is able to respond to problems that confront an increasing number of homeless Americans.

The Westchester County and Pinellas County experiences are becoming more and more common among the nation's 3,042 counties. The growth in demands for services from county governments, although not even, has transformed many counties into full-service local governments.

This chapter focuses in four ways on the growing service role of American counties. First, an explanation is provided for *why* counties have become more significant producers of public services. Second, we detail the growth in county services using fiscal data about *all* counties in the

United States. Third, the expanding service role of *urban* counties is documented and discussed. Fourth, changes in the service scope of counties in a rapid growth state—Florida—are presented and examined. To provide additional perspective, county service roles are compared and contrasted with municipal service roles for the years 1975 to 1988.

COUNTIES AS SERVICE PROVIDERS

Increasing numbers of counties are providing municipal or urban-like services. Services such as parks and recreation, libraries, refuse collection and solid waste disposal, fire protection, planning and zoning, airports, emergency medical care, environmental protection, and economic development are being supplied in greater numbers by counties. Indeed, this situation has led one observer to conclude that "a wide array of new responsibilities by counties fulfilling the role of 'urban service providers' has elevated the importance of counties in an increasingly complex service-delivery structure" (Todd, 1991).

What is behind the expanding service role of counties? There are at least three major influences: urbanization, suburbanization, and modernization.

The United States has become an increasingly urban nation over the past century. This trend has caused 27 cities and counties to consolidate their governments in order to provide more services in a cost-effective fashion. In other instances, cities and counties have contracted with one another or cooperated in other ways to coordinate efforts and programs in response to urban service demands.

More than anything else, urbanization has meant that urban service issues are no longer confined to municipalities. They are increasingly county, or even metropolitan, issues. For instance, city responsibility for solid and hazardous waste or sewage may end with collection, but the county typically is expected to be responsible for disposal or treatment. Another example is law enforcement. Except for trial appearances, the responsibility of city police often ends at booking. The county must then feed, house, clothe, medicate, adjudicate, prosecute, defend, and supervise most offenders returned to the community. Moreover, a whole host of issues, ranging from pollution control to transportation to emergency medical care, are countywide (and in some instances metropolitanwide) in scope and, hence, warrant a response from a government with areawide jurisdiction.

Suburbanization also has had an influence on the expanding service role of counties. Suburban dwellers are turning in increasing numbers to county government for services and desired amenities. In fact, Schneider and Park

(1989) conclude that county governments are "the front-line government for the large proportion of suburban residents who live in unincorporated areas of metropolitan regions." These "non-cities," sometimes referred to as "megacounties," can be found near Chicago (DuPage County), Washington, D.C. (Fairfax County, Virginia), Atlanta (Cobb County), and other places.

Growth in unincorporated America between 1980 and 1990 registered a 9 percent gain compared to an 8 percent gain in incorporated America. In rapid-growth states like Florida, the population growth in unincorporated areas has been much more dramatic. Between 1980 and 1990, Florida's population increased 33 percent. Some 64 percent of this growth occurred in unincorporated areas, while 36 percent occurred in cities. Stated differently, there was a 22 percent population increase in the incorporated areas and a 45 percent increase in the unincorporated areas. In fact, 51 percent of Florida's population currently resides outside the state's municipalities. This growth pattern has prompted one analyst to describe Florida as a "large sprawling, single-family suburban subdivision" (Meier, 1991, B1).

County modernization has also aided in the adoption and provision of urban-type services. In many states, counties have been granted home-rule powers that enable them to be more autonomous and vigorous in responding to public demands. Since the early 1900s, 36 states have relinquished control over counties and, through the grant of home-rule powers, have given counties more discretionary authority (T. Salant, 1988b). At the same time, counties are moving toward greater centralization of executive and policy-making authority. This is evidenced by the fact that 786 counties have installed the commission-administrator form of government (Jeffery et al., 1989), which is a variation of the council-manager plan widely employed by municipalities. Another 383 counties have opted for an elected executive form of government, somewhat similar to that in place in Westchester County, New York (Jeffery et al., 1989). Other modernization efforts include centralizing procurement practices and adopting sophisticated accounting procedures. These measures have strengthened the ability of counties to provide more services and, presumably, better service.

Despite these developments, there is little documentation available to determine just how the scope of county services is changing or the direction it is taking.[1] However, some fiscal data are available that permit useful comparisons to be made, especially between counties and cities.

COUNTY AND MUNICIPAL SERVICE EXPENDITURES

Local government in the United States is big business. The nation's 3,042 counties spent $32.7 billion in FY 1975 and $105.5 billion in FY 1988 to provide services to their residents.[2] During this 13-year period, county government expenditures increased 223 percent. Municipal expenditures increased from $48.7 billion to $133.9 billion, a 175 percent increase.

Other expenditure data provide a different perspective on county government services. Per capita expenditures facilitate comparisons between counties and municipalities and provide a measure of size and effort. Per capita *county* expenditures, not surprisingly, have been less than those for municipalities. For instance, counties spent $176 and $475 per person in FY 1975 and FY 1988, respectively, while municipalities spent $359 and $893 per person during these same fiscal years. Per capita expenditures in current dollars increased 170 percent and 149 percent, respectively, for counties and municipalities between FY 1975 and FY 1988. Moreover, the ratio of county expenditures to municipal expenditures increased from 49.1 percent in FY 1975 to 53.2 percent in FY 1988.

The percentage of money dedicated to various services tells another story about what county governments do and do not do. In particular, these data reflect the emphasis placed on various services. Seven broad categories of services can be helpful in this regard:[3]

General Governmental—includes expenditures for legislative, executive, financial, administrative, judicial and legal, court reporting/recording, and general public buildings construction and maintenance activities and services.

Public Safety—includes expenditures for law enforcement, fire control, detention/correction, relief services, ambulance and rescue services, medical examiner, and consumer affairs activities and services.

Physical Environment—includes expenditures for electric, water, and gas utility, garbage collection and solid waste disposal, sewers, conservation and resource management, and flood control activities and services.

Transportation—includes expenditures for road and street facilities, airports, water transportation systems, transit systems, and parking facilities.

Economic Development—includes expenditures for employment opportunity and development, industry development, veterans affairs, and housing and urban development activities and services.

Human Services—includes expenditures for hospitals, health, mental health, and retardation services.

Culture/Recreation—includes expenditures for libraries, parks and recreation, cultural services, special events, and special recreation facilities.

Figure 5.1 shows that Human Services and Economic Development were the top priorities of county governments in both FY 1975 and FY 1988, although the ranks were reversed in FY 1988. In fact, more than one out of every five county dollars were spent for Human Services in FY 1975 and FY 1988. Counties also devoted considerable resources to General Government and Transportation, the third and fourth priorities, respectively, during FY 1975. By FY 1988, counties were placing greater emphasis on Public Safety and Physical Environment. This increased emphasis means that some problem areas received smaller shares of service expenditures in FY 1988 when compared to FY 1975. This was particularly the case for Economic Development and Transportation services.

An examination of the spending priorities assigned by the 19,205 municipalities in the United States to the same expenditures categories show several differences (see Figure 5.2). The largest proportion of municipal expenditures in both fiscal years was dedicated to the Physical Environment (e.g., electric, water, and gas utilities; natural resources; sewage, sanitation, solid waste; etc.). Spending for Public Safety was the second priority. Municipalities also devoted considerably smaller proportions of their budgets to Human Services, Economic Development, and General Government.

Differences between counties and municipalities appear to be largely the result of differences in responsibilities. Counties, for example, have many health/welfare and judicial responsibilities that cities do not have. Thus the numbers in the Human Services and General Government categories are larger for counties.

Several expenditure patterns suggest that the service role of counties is becoming more similar to that of municipalities. First, both aggregate and per capita county expenditures are increasing at a faster pace than expenditures of municipalities and, therefore, are rapidly "catching up" with municipal spending levels. Second, the proportion of county expenditures allocated to Public Safety and Physical Environment increased between FY 1975 and FY 1988. These two categories contain services historically recognized as belonging to municipalities (e.g., police and fire protection, ambulance and rescue services, protective inspections and regulations,

Figure 5.1
All Counties

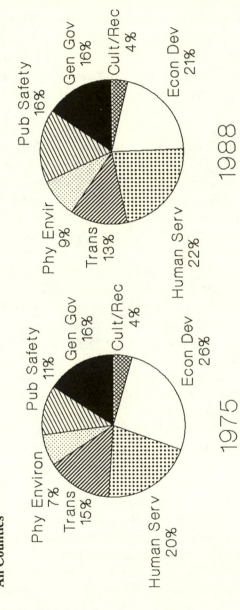

1975

Pub Safety
11%

Phy Environ
7%

Trans
15%

Gen Gov
16%

Cult/Rec
4%

Econ Dev
26%

Human Serv
20%

1988

Pub Safety
16%

Phy Envir
9%

Trans
13%

Gen Gov
16%

Cult/Rec
4%

Econ Dev
21%

Human Serv
22%

Figure 5.2
All Municipalities

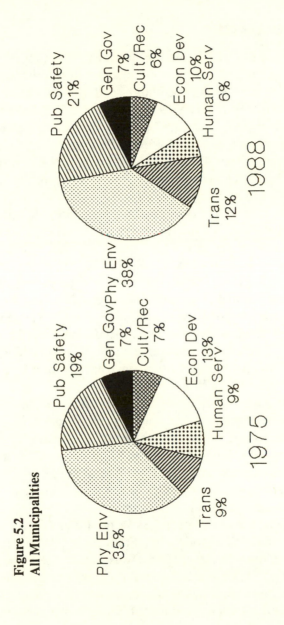

Pub Safety
19%

Gen Gov
7%

Phy Env
38%

Cult/Rec
7%

Econ Dev
13%

Human Serv
9%

Trans
9%

Phy Env
35%

1975

Pub Safety
21%

Gen Gov
7%

Cult/Rec
6%

Econ Dev
10%

Human Serv
6%

Trans
12%

1988

electric/gas/water utilities, garbage collection, solid waste management,
and sewage collection and treatment).

URBAN COUNTIES

The service role and activity of urban counties (defined here as those
with populations of 100,000 or more) also can be profiled by examining
aggregate and per capita expenditures and spending priorities. Expenditures by urban counties in FY 1975 amounted to $22.8 billion; in FY 1988,
this figure had jumped to $75.7 billion. Over this 13-year span, county
spending increased 232 percent. Municipal spending for the same time
frame increased from $31.7 billion to $83.6, a 164 percent increase. In
short, the difference between urban county expenditures and municipal
expenditures had narrowed by FY 1988.

Per capita expenditures show that urban counties do not exert the same
effort as urban municipalities in providing services. Urban counties spent
$167 and $455 per person in FY 1975 and FY 1988, respectively, whereas
urban municipalities spent $397 and $1,003 per capita during the same
fiscal years. A closer inspection of these figures indicates that urban
counties began to make a greater effort over this period. For example, per
capita expenditures for urban counties increased 173 percent between FY
1975 and FY 1988, while per capita expenditures for urban municipalities
increased 153 percent. In addition, the ratio of urban county expenditures
to urban municipality expenditures increased from 42.1 percent to 45.4
percent between FY 1975 and FY 1988.

An examination of spending priorities sheds additional light on the
changing service role of urban counties (see Figure 5.3). Urban counties
devoted the largest proportion of their fiscal resources to Economic
Development and Human Services in FY 1975. Services in these categories remained top priorities in FY 1988, although the rank order was
reversed. By 1988, urban counties were spending more on Public Safety,
Physical Environment, and Transportation. As a consequence, less emphasis was placed on funding services in the Economic Development and
Culture/Recreation categories. In all probability, the decline in emphasis
placed on Economic Development was due to the decrease in federal
funding for public welfare, while the lower priority given to Culture/Rec-
reation may have been due to declines in demands in those urban counties
that have built a sufficient number of libraries and parks and recreational
facilities.

The spending priorities of urban municipalities, although different in
some respects, show a greater similarity to spending priorities of urban

Figure 5.3
All Counties over 100,000

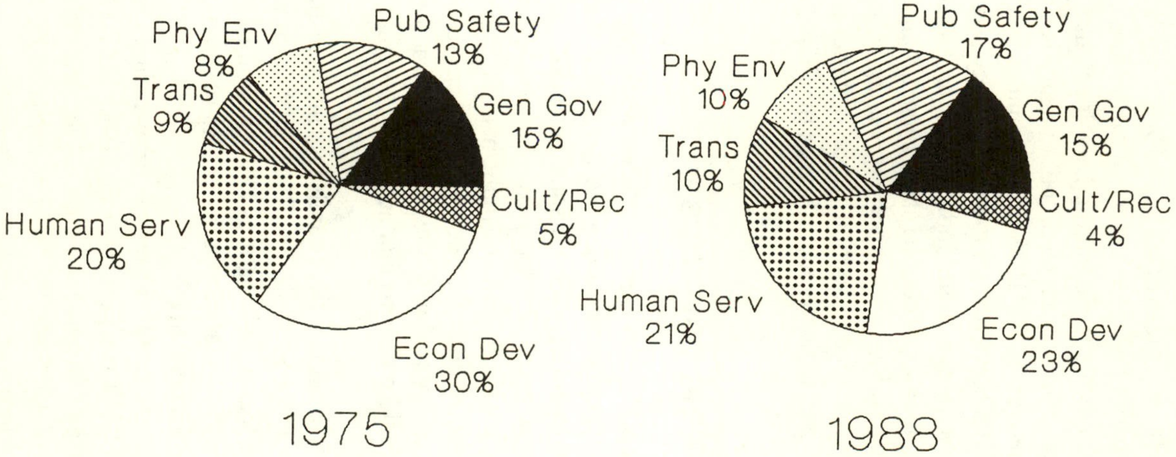

1975

Human Serv
20%

Econ Dev
30%

Cult/Rec
5%

Gen Gov
15%

Pub Safety
13%

Phy Env
8%

Trans
9%

1988

Human Serv
21%

Econ Dev
23%

Cult/Rec
4%

Gen Gov
15%

Pub Safety
17%

Phy Env
10%

Trans
10%

counties (see Figure 5.4). Like municipalities in general, urban municipalities assigned a higher priority to services in the Physical Environment category and placed less emphasis on services in the Human Services and General Government areas in both FY 1975 and FY 1988. Unlike municipalities in general, however, urban municipalities devoted larger shares of the expenditure pie to Economic Development services in both fiscal years. In fact, the priority given to this category is similar to that of urban counties. Moreover, by FY 1988 urban counties and urban municipalities allocated roughly equal dollars to Public Safety services.

All in all, two things would indicate that urban counties are becoming more like their municipal counterparts. First, urban counties are spending more dollars on both an aggregate and per capita basis to provide public services to their residents. Second, urban counties are assigning a higher priority to services typically identified as municipal responsibilities.

FAST-GROWING COUNTIES

Florida is a high-growth state. It is currently the third fastest growing state in terms of actual numbers of new residents, trailing only California and Texas. Approximately 893 persons move to the state every day, which, when totaled, exceeds 325,000 new residents every year. This sizable migration, along with growth due to the natural birth rate, has transformed many rural counties into urban centers. As a consequence, many counties in Florida are confronted with the challenge of addressing new problems or dealing with old problems that have grown in magnitude and complexity.

In FY 1975, Florida's 67 counties spent $1.9 billion, while its 390 municipalities spent $2.5 billion. By FY 1988, however, counties were spending more than municipalities ($9.9 billion to $7.2 billion). County expenditures also increased at a faster rate (421 percent) than municipal expenditures (188 percent).

A similar pattern can be observed for per capita expenditures. Florida counties spent $114 per person in FY 1975 and $844 per person in FY 1988, a whopping 640 percent increase. Florida municipalities spent $509 per capita in FY 1975 and $1,143 per capita in FY 1988, a modest 188 percent gain. Moreover, the ratio of county per capita expenditures to municipal per capita expenditures increased from a meager 22.4 percent in FY 1975 to 73.8 percent in FY 1988. In sum, the service role of the typical Florida county, as reflected by these numbers, is growing at a faster pace than counties nationwide or even urban counties, in general.

Figure 5.4
All Municipalities over 100,000

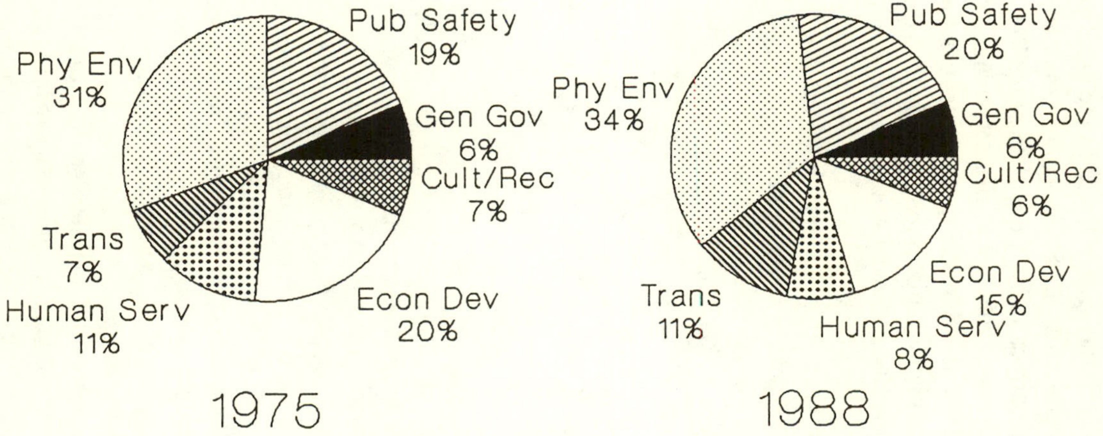

1975

1988

Figure 5.5 reveals that the largest proportions of Florida county expenditures are allocated to services in the General Government, Public Safety, Physical Environment, and Transportation categories. General Government was the top priority of Florida counties in FY 1975. By FY 1988, however, Public Safety had emerged as the number-one priority.

Figure 5.6 shows that the Physical Environment was the top priority of Florida municipalities in both FY 1975 and FY 1988. Public Safety and General Government placed a distant second and third, respectively. Between FY 1975 and FY 1988, municipalities devoted larger shares of the expenditure pie to Public Safety and Culture/Recreation, while reducing proportions allocated to Physical Environment and General Government.

The Florida case suggests that the service roles of counties in fast-growth states are likely to resemble the service roles of municipalities. Indeed, counties in Florida spend more money in total for services than do municipalities and are rapidly catching up with municipalities in terms of per capita spending. In addition, the priorities that Florida counties assign to four categories of services (Public Safety, Economic Development, Culture/Recreation, and General Government) are similar to the priorities assigned to these services by municipalities.

SUMMARY

This analysis has shown that the service role of many counties is approaching in scope and magnitude the service role of municipalities. This is particularly the case for urban counties in high growth areas. Aggregate and per capita county spending for services is increasing at a faster pace than that for municipalities. In addition, counties are allocating a larger proportion of their expenditures to Public Safety, Physical Environment, Transportation, and Culture/Recreation services. In other words, counties are assigning a higher priority to urban-type services such as police and fire protection, emergency medical care, water service, and environmental protection.

A closer inspection of the service role of all U.S. counties, urban counties, and fast-growing counties helps to bring things into sharper focus (see Figure 5.7). There is a great deal of similarity between all counties and urban counties with respect to the priority they assign to each of the seven categories of services. Service priorities of fast-growing counties (like those in Florida), however, differ from all counties nationwide and urban counties in two basic ways. First, fast-growing counties allocate substantially larger expenditure shares to Public Safety, Transportation,

Figure 5.5
All Counties in Florida

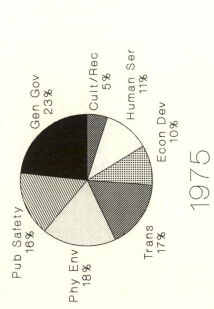

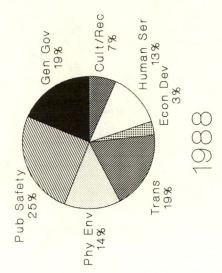

Figure 5.6
All Municipalities in Florida

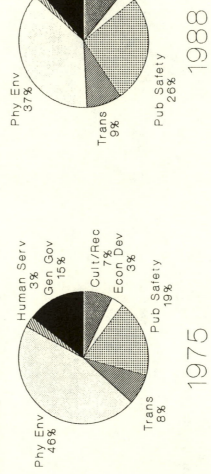

Human Serv 3%
Gen Gov 15%
Cult/Rec 7%
Econ Dev 3%
Pub Safety 19%
Trans 8%
Phy Env 46%

1975

Human Serv 2%
Gen Gov 12%
Cult/Rec 11%
Econ Dev 3%
Pub Safety 26%
Trans 9%
Phy Env 37%

1988

Figure 5.7
County Services by Function, 1988

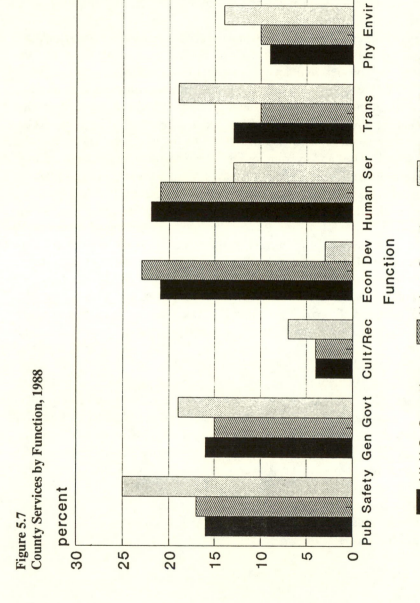

Sources: U.S. Census Bureau; County Government Finances; City Government Finances; Florida Comptroller's
Office; Local Government Financial Report, 1988.

and Physical Environment. Growth clearly creates demands for more and better police and fire protection, roads and highways, sewer and water lines, and the like. Second, they devote considerably less money than their counterparts in slow-growth regions to Economic Development and Human Services.

Regardless of the manner in which expenditure data are analyzed, the general conclusion is the same: Counties are expanding their service delivery capabilities and are providing more and more services that, historically, were provided only by municipal governments. This trend is likely to continue into the 1990s and beyond. Growth in the service role of counties, however, is not likely to occur uniformly. Still, it should be most pronounced in two settings. First, it is likely to take place in high-growth states and in counties with large numbers of persons residing in unincorporated areas. During the past several decades, most population increases in rapid-growth states have occurred in unincorporated areas. As the size of the unincorporated population increases and takes on an increasingly urban character, greater demands will be placed on counties to provide a wider menu of urban-type services. In short, county governments are quickly becoming the front-line service providers for the large proportion of residents who live in unincorporated areas of counties.

Second, services are likely to be added in those counties that house municipalities with growing populations but slowly expanding, perhaps static, tax bases, where alternative sources of revenue are limited, and federal and state fiscal aid are shrinking. Under these circumstances, municipal residents may well demand that the responsibility for some services (e.g., solid waste disposal management, parks and recreational facilities and activities, land use control, regulation of water and air quality, sewage treatment, etc.) be transferred to counties. Stated differently, counties can be expected to provide an expanding assortment of services to those who reside in municipalities because county governments remain "administrative arms" of the state and serve as areawide governments with vital linking and coordinating responsibilities.

In conclusion, these growing duties and responsibilities as well as others described in this chapter may make the American county *the* local government of the 1990s.

NOTES

1. The increasingly important service role of counties has gained the attention of a few students of urban government in recent years (Duncombe, 1977;

DeGrove and Lawrence, 1977; Benton and Rigos, 1985; Oakerson, Parks, and Bell, 1987; Schneider and Park, 1989; Benton and Menzel, 1991a and 1991b).

2. These figures, as well as those that follow for urban counties and counties in Florida, do not include expenditures by special districts. It is impossible to separate out expenditures provided by municipal-oriented districts and county-oriented special districts.

3. Debt service expenditures and expenditures listed as "other financing uses" are excluded from the analysis that follows.

Chapter 6

Metropolitan Counties and Urbanization

Vincent L. Marando and C. Douglas Baker

The metropolitan arena is being transformed. This transformation is taking the form of a massive, if piecemeal, reconcentration of the population away from urban cores to their peripheries. This process has occurred slowly and disjointedly but the results are dramatic and clear. Urban America is no longer personified by an economically and politically dominant core city with dependent zones at its periphery (Fishman, 1987, 1990). Contemporary urban America is one in which the periphery is becoming increasingly independent—economically, politically, and even socially—from the once-predominant center city. As a result of the massive population shift from the core to the periphery, county governments in metropolitan areas have taken on an extremely important role in policy-making and service delivery.

An example of the growing importance of counties is the increase in the number of counties designated as being within Metropolitan Statistical Areas by the Census Bureau. To obtain metropolitan status, a county must include a central city with a population of at least 50,000. In addition, social and economic standards based on residential, employment, and commuting patterns among local units are used to determine the metropolitan status of counties.[1] As Table 6.1 shows, the number of counties in MSAs has risen from 310 in 1962 to 735 in 1987, which represents an increase of over 137 percent. The number of municipalities in MSAs during the same time period rose more than 80 percent (4,142 to 7,488), while special districts in MSAs more than doubled (5,411 to 12,690). Since the total number of counties has remained basically the same since 1962,

County Governments

Table 6.1
Units of Government Inside and Outside Metropolitan Statistical Areas,
1962–87

	Inside MSAs				Outside MSAs			
YEAR	1962	1972	1977	1987	1962	1972	1977	1987
COUNTY	310	444	594	735	2733	2600	2448	2307
MUNIC.	4142	5467	6444	7488	13855	13050	12418	11712
TOWNSP.	2575	3462	4031	5036	14569	13529	12791	11655
SDs	5411	8054	9580	12690	12912	15831	16382	16842

Source: Census of Governments 1967, 1972, 1977, 1987.

it is clear that this increase represents existing counties that have met the criteria for being designated as metropolitan.

Today there are 738 counties in metropolitan America. These counties contain about 76 percent of the nation's population (Fosler, 1991). There is wide agreement that counties are assuming greater roles in resolving problems created by urban populations (Duncombe, 1977; Sharp, 1990). Counties are raising more resources, incurring larger expenditures, engaging in more regulatory activities, employing more personnel, and assuming greater service delivery commitments. Counties are increasingly responding to the demands generated by metropolitanization. Behind the county's expanding role in metropolitan areas, however, is a great deal of variety and diversity.

In this chapter we spell out the complex landscape of metropolitan counties and urbanization. That landscape involves the patterns of growth and development that are influencing county governments in various ways both internally (revenues, expenditures, service responsibilities, debt) and externally (networks of local governments, county-state and county-national relationships).

Although metropolitan status is important in understanding change in county government, additional factors also need to be examined. We believe that the effects of metropolitanization on counties are not sufficient to explain contemporary county government. We analyze and discuss, along with metropolitan status, several factors that aid in presenting a comprehensive picture of the changing roles of metropolitan counties. The chapter concludes with observations and discussion on the evolving role of counties in metropolitan areas, particularly its potential for meeting urban needs and equalizing services among diverse populations.

COUNTIES AND THE METROPOLITAN CONTEXT

Metropolitan county governments have faced tremendous growth, especially in the 1970s and 1980s (Richter, 1985). As the recently released 1990 Census figures show, this process continues at a rapid pace. Indeed, the *Washington Post* notes that suburban counties around Washington, D.C. "are growing at the pace of Third World countries," while the District's population is declining (Fehr and Cohn, 1990). As the urban environment expands, adjacent suburbs are becoming much like the central city. The *Los Angeles Times* proclaims that some of Los Angeles' adjacent suburbs are currently or are rapidly becoming the "new slums" (J. Stewart, 1990). Similar trends have been shown to exist in other major urban areas (Vobejda, 1990; Logan and Schneider, 1984). Thus, units of government in these areas, including counties, have become very important players in the allocation of resources and services and in dealing with problems of rapid growth and urban decline.

Urban deconcentration in the 1980s followed a fairly consistent pattern and was institutionalized by many factors. First, shopping malls, convenience stores, fast-food restaurants, and other conveniences have followed the populace into suburban county areas. Manufacturing and office jobs have also moved into the urban fringe. Mass manufacturing requiring large tracts of land, inexpensive rental space for offices, and an available pool of manpower have all contributed to the solidification of the suburban movement (Kasarda, 1978). In fact, suburban governments now compete with each other, as well as with the central city, for the location of firms with potentially large numbers of jobs.

The most dynamic conceptualization of the suburbanization process is offered by Frisbie and Kasarda (1988, 651):

> Non-metropolitan growth entails the spread of urban organization across the entire society. In other words, expansion of interstate highways, extension of public utilities (including electrical power, water, and telephone lines), telecommunications advances (especially television cable and satellite disks), and the society-wide availability of standardized goods and services means that no sector of society is without urban amenities and opportunities.

The perspective taken here is that suburbanization, specifically the movement of populations further from the central city into adjacent counties, is an ongoing process. Even if the process slows, central cities will be unlikely to gain population (Downs, 1973, 1985). Population shifts will occur within suburban county areas around the central cities. As a result, the study of urban areas inevitably includes the expanding role of county governments in metropolitan areas.

Metropolitan counties are rapidly growing and politics often center around growth and development. For example, economic development, especially involving large nonretail firms and high-density dwellings, will create conflict among residents. Transportation policies, including the construction or extension of highways and mass transit, are also critical community issues as they relate to access among suburbs, and from suburbs to the central city.

Daniel Garnick (1988) classified counties by their spatial relationship to the central city and population size. We have modified this classification to describe the context of metropolitan counties. The four categories of counties include: (1) "core counties" that contain the central city and its surrounding suburban jurisdictions (i.e., Wayne County, Detroit, Michigan) or counties that contain part of the central city and have populations of at least 1 million people; (2) "core contiguous" counties including adjacent suburbs (i.e. Montgomery County, Maryland); (3) "noncore contiguous counties" that have populations of greater than 250,000 or intermediate suburbs (i.e. Anne Arundel County, Maryland); and (4) "noncore contiguous" counties with less than 250,000 population (i.e. Stafford County, Virginia) (Garnick, 1988).

Generally, the core county overlays the central city and suburban municipalities. The central city remains a diverse entity with central business districts, manufacturing, and a variety of shopping areas. Core counties are dominated by high-density dwellings with high concentrations of low- to moderate-income groups, especially in the fringes. There are also wealthy enclaves within central cities and core counties.

Counties adjacent to the core county have similar problems and demographic makeup. They may have "spillover" effects from the central city with many of the problems common to poor, immobile populations. These include high-density dwellings and population, poor housing stock, high crime, and heavy traffic congestion (Logan and Schneider, 1984). These counties also have lower-middle class/middle-class neighborhoods with easy access and proximity to the central city. They may, however, also have many rural traits depending on their size and diversity.

The intermediate counties provide a desirable housing location for middle- and upper-income residents. These counties are often served by mass transit systems or major highways. They also include a high proportion of affluent residents with access to shopping areas and malls and contain a high proportion of single-family dwellings and townhouses. The population tends to be upper middle class and affluent. These counties allow easy access to the central city and other communities, while providing many suburban amenities, such as lower density dwellings, proximate shopping areas, and low crime neighborhoods.

Finally, the outer ring of counties comprising the metropolitan hinterland are also desirable locations because housing is more affordable and there is abundant open space. Residents of these areas, however, lack easy access to the central city and other urban amenities. The hinterland counties will be populated by the middle class to wealthy in low-density housing such as single-family dwellings, townhouses, and luxury homes. Residents also pay high transportation costs in time and money, but this is balanced by the amenities of open space, affordable housing, and homogeneity of middle-class life-styles. These suburban counties usually pursue policies to attract wealthy residents. Real estate agents and developers are often catalysts for rapidly expanding the construction rate of new homes and higher density dwellings in urban fringe counties (Logan and Molotch, 1987). As a result, the hinterland counties have experienced high rates of population growth and increases in housing density, roads, and service costs. The hinterland counties will be the next-generation "intermediate counties" as urbanization continues to affect these areas.

ATLANTA MSA: AN EXAMPLE OF CHANGE

The Atlanta Metropolitan Statistical Area is an excellent example of the dynamics associated with urbanization and county government (see Table 6.2). The entire Atlanta metropolitan area has rapidly gained population, growing from 1,390,164 in 1970 to 2,833,511 in 1990, a rate of 103.8 percent over the 20-year period. Meanwhile, the city of Atlanta lost population, dropping from 496,973 to 394,017, a net loss of 20.7 percent. The population gains in Atlanta's metropolitan area were primarily in suburban counties and municipalities. In fact, the city of Atlanta represented 49 percent of the population of the Atlanta MSA in 1950 but only 14 percent in 1990. While this drop is primarily a result of the increased number of counties in the Atlanta MSA, a similar drop occurred between 1980 and 1990 from 21 to 14 percent, respectively. The Atlanta MSA has grown from 3 counties in 1950 to 18 counties in 1990, creating a decentralized and sprawling urban area. Growth in the Atlanta MSA has primarily followed the major transportation routes, especially interstate highways (Hirsch, 1987).

Figure 6.1 shows the Atlanta MSA's 18 counties (which have not changed in number since 1983). In general, the counties' demographic

Table 6.2
Atlanta MSA and the City of Atlanta, 1950–90

ATLANTA MSA	1950	1960	1970	1980	1990*
Number of Counties	3	5	5	15	18
Total Population	671,797	1,017,188	1,390,164	2,029,710	2,833,511
% Change Previous Census		33.9	68.6	79.7	39.6
CITY OF ATLANTA					
Population	331,314	487,455	496,973	425,022	394,017
% Change Previous Census Population		47.1	2.0	-14.5	-7.3
Percent of total MSA (rounded)	49	48	36	21	14

* 1990 Figures subject to change.

Source: Adapted from data compiled by Paul Hirsch, Georgia State University, from Census Bureau data. Used with permission.

characteristics follow the urban-suburban pattern described above. There are, of course, exceptions. Similar to the Atlanta MSA, most metropolitan areas are growing substantially outside the center city and in metropolitan county areas. As a result, the number of counties classified as being metropolitan has increased too. Metropolitan counties within specific MSAs often vary by size, population, and other demographic variables. Metropolitan counties also contain an array of governmental units and varying numbers of people who live in unincorporated areas. In sum, residents of metropolitan areas do not necessarily live in large counties, nor in localities with urban infrastructure (e.g., mass transit; high-density dwellings). Rather, metropolitan counties exhibit variety in size, local governmental arrangements, and commitment to services.

Further, the fourfold typology and the Atlanta example mask a great deal of intracounty variation. Metropolitan counties, regardless of population size, face diversity of demands and problems. For example, there are large variations between metropolitan counties as to the percentage of the population living in unincorporated areas. Whether residents live in municipalities or unincorporated areas affects the types and level of services the county provides. Further, many large metropolitan counties may contain "spillover" suburbs, intermediate suburbs, and rural-like "hinterland" areas all within their jurisdiction. Different areas of a county

Figure 6.1
Development of the Atlanta MSA

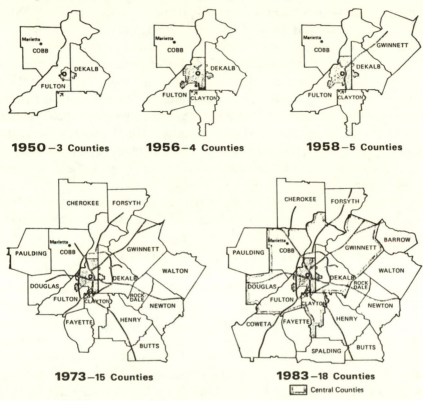

1950 –3 Counties   1956 –4 Counties   1958 –5 Counties

1973 –15 Counties   1983 –18 Counties

Source: Hirsch (1987). Used with permission.

may require different sets of services and assistance. Finally, even metropolitan counties with small populations facing rapid change must address a variety of "urban" issues that are new and unfamiliar to public officials. A key to understanding the concerns and issues of importance to metropolitan county governments goes beyond simply viewing them as independent governmental units. They exist in a rapidly changing urban environment whose problems are metropolitan in scope—despite their diversity.

COUNTY SERVICES IN METROPOLITAN AREAS

In general, large metropolitan counties raise more revenues per capita and have higher expenditures per capita than smaller counties. Metropol-

itan counties also assume more service obligations than their nonmetropolitan counterparts. This finding is not surprising and has been pointed
out in several studies (Duncombe, 1977; Benton and Menzel, 1990). What
should also be noted is the wide variation among metropolitan counties in
their levels of revenues, expenditures, and service commitments.

The average per capita revenues and expenditures for metropolitan
counties in 1987 were $589 and $568, respectively. The metropolitan
county with the highest per capita revenues and expenditures is Fairfax
County, Virginia, at $2,092 and $1,925, respectively. By contrast, the
lowest per capita revenues and expenditures is Essex County, Massachusetts, at $41 and $39, respectively. These examples illustrate the vast range
in the revenues, expenditures, and service commitments made by metropolitan counties.

Despite wide variation in the level and types of services metropolitan
counties provide, there are two primary clusters of services that can be
identified. Many counties in metropolitan areas provide a two-tiered
service delivery system (see Table 6.3). All residents are eligible to receive
the "top tier" of services, which includes services provided to all county
residents (J. Thomas, 1987). The second tier of services are subarea
specific. Only residents of certain geographic subareas of the counties pay
for and are entitled to receive these selected services, such as sewers,
sidewalks, and street lights. It is the metropolitan county's transformation
into a two-tiered service delivery local government that has allowed
counties a means to respond to the demands of urbanizing populations and
fulfill their state-imposed service obligations. The services listed in Table
6.3 are classified according to top tier (areawide) and bottom tier (area-
specific).

Top-Tier Services

Metropolitan counties provide areawide services that are often "urban"
in character, such as parks and recreation, libraries, professional police
protection, economic and community development, and pollution control.
As counties have grown in population and have become metropolitan, they
have provided "urban-type" services to all their residents, many of whom
were former city residents and have become accustomed to city services.
Less affluent county residents are entitled to the same services as more
affluent residents and taxpayers. Therefore counties equalize service provision of top-tier services. To the extent there are great variations in income
among county residents, the redistribution may be quite significant. Since
counties also include urban and suburban populations, the redistributive

Table 6.3
County Services: Countywide and County Subarea

Countywide or "Top Tier" *	County Subarea or "Bottom Tier"
Public Health	Residential Streets
Hospitals	Water and Sewers
Welfare	Fire Protection
Corrections	Police
Roads	Solid Waste Disposal
Libraries	Regional Library**
Police	Street Lights
Fire	Health
Emergency Medical Services	Pest/Mosquito Control
Parks and Recreation	Parking
Education	Community Centers
Water and Sewers	Irrigation
Land Fills	Weed Control
	Special Districts***

*   Services can be provided at both levels simultaneously
-- budgetary analysis rarely displays the level of service
delivery complexity.

**   Region refers to a portion of a county, for example,
Western Howard County Maryland. Region is not in reference
to a multicounty area.

*** Multiple uses of special districts include sewage,
drainage, street lighting, parks and recreation, flood
control, water supply, solid waste disposal, libraries,
fire protection, and so on.

aspects of county service delivery may be much more dramatic than that
provided exclusively within cities.

Some areawide services, such as public health, hospitals, and welfare,
are explicitly redistributive in nature and are often assigned by the state to
the counties. Although all residents do not receive public welfare, residents
are not excluded because of where they live within the county or what they
pay in taxes. Further, many county services are entitlement services and
not distributed to individuals based on ability to pay.

Bottom-Tier Services

Counties are increasingly providing services to the populations of
geographic subareas. These services are often not mandated by state
governments. Rather, states may "allow" counties to provide these services in response to resident demand. John Thomas (1987), former executive director of the National Association of Counties, has identified them

as "quality of life" services, which in many ways parallel the "urban" services provided by municipalities. These may include water, sewer, sanitation, garbage collection, fire protection, street lighting, and residential street construction and maintenance. These services are those that are generally related to the general urban character of an area when measured by population size and density groupings of the county.

Twenty-two states have granted counties the authority to create service districts for a specific subarea of the county (U.S. Bureau of the Census, 1988 vol. 1). Metropolitan counties in many states have such subarea service districts to provide a variety of services in response to residents' demands. A significant feature of services provided by these subarea service districts is that only the residents who receive the services pay for them. These functional services—such as water systems, sewers, and fire protection—are often financed by an assessment against the property in the area or through a fee or user charge. The general county property tax base is not used for financing bottom-tier services.

Many counties of metropolitan America are providing expanded area-wide and area-specific services to meet a multiplicity of citizen needs. Counties remain administrative units in the delivery of many services, especially those assigned by the state; however, this state administrative role is changing. Metropolitan counties often raise the quality of the state-mandated services beyond a state's minimum requirements in response to the expectations of former city residents. Whereas county-wide services are financed by taxes and often equalize what citizens receive, the bottom-tiered services are not intended to provide equity in service delivery. Rather, residents are offered an opportunity to meet their local needs without transferring financial burden to the entire county's population.

County Service Evolution: Potential for Redistribution

Paul Peterson (1981), in *City Limits*, maintains that redistributive services (such as health, hospitals, and public welfare) are less likely to be pursued by cities than the state and federal governments. The reason, it is argued, is that services such as health care derive revenue from all residents but primarily benefit the less affluent and less politically active portion of the population. This argument must be used with extreme caution when assessing metropolitan county governments. These jurisdictions are spending a substantial amount of their budgets on redistributive services (health, hospitals, public welfare). According to Robert Ebel (1991, 14), "the single most important function of counties is social services and income maintenance." In 1988, counties spent 29.1 percent of their budget on social welfare and income maintenance (Ebel, 1991). Schneider and Park (1989) found a sharp contrast in redistributive expenditures between suburban municipalities and counties in metropolitan areas, with counties consistently spending greater amounts on these services. Their study suggests that counties are providing redistributive services such as health, hospitals, and public welfare, while municipalities are more likely to provide developmental services such as transportation and infrastructure. To further support this important county role, Sharp (1990, 139) found that "county governments are even more likely to be involved in the delivery of redistributive social services [than cities]."

County governments have more potential than cities to address the issues of service equity and redistribution between the affluent and poor residents. This potential is a result of county government's unique position in the local governmental network in metropolitan areas. Counties, especially those in metropolitan areas, serve larger geographic regions and more diverse populations than do municipalities, including those in central cities. Therefore, many metropolitan counties have a broader tax base and greater ability than cities to pursue policies that equalize burdens and service provision. Further, most counties have been mandated by states to provide health and public welfare services and have the administrative and organizational experience to deliver such services efficiently. Finally, where counties provide services such as police, fire, public transportation, and such, they are generally obligated to provide service to residents equitably. Counties are directly in the business of tax and service redistribution among affluent and less affluent residents.

The aggressiveness and extent to which metropolitan counties can pursue redistributive policies depends on a number of factors. First, counties as administrative arms of state governments are limited in their taxing and spending authority. Most states have mandated county governments to provide redistributive services but left them little discretion in raising revenues for such services (J. Thomas, 1987). The increasing fiscal stress facing central cities and municipalities inhibits them from providing adequate service levels, shifting some of this burden to counties. In response, many metropolitan counties may be providing higher levels of services with redistributive effects. Second, given expanding tax bases and increased fiscal authority, county governments do have the potential to address issues of service equality in metropolitan areas where central cities and some suburbs are more fiscally strained.

Growth and Debt: Another Service?

Among the many consequences of population growth for metropolitan counties is the increasing need for building infrastructure and public facilities to accommodate resident needs. Population growth requires new transportation systems, expanding existing roads and highways, constructing adequate water and sewer systems, erecting public buildings to house larger administrations, and increasing numbers of public employees. Counties often borrow in response to the service demands of middle-income residents requesting "quality of life" services such as libraries, parks and recreation facilities, and residential streets. Growth not only generates resources, it also requires massive public commitments and expenditures that often cannot be met entirely from current operating budgets.

Many metropolitan counties are borrowing revenues to finance the capital expenditures needed to construct infrastructure and public facilities. In many cases interest payment on debt has become a major expenditure along with provision of more traditional services. Payment of interest to retire county debt increased from less than 2 percent of general expenditures in 1967 to approximately 7 percent in 1988 (Ebel, 1991).

Large counties borrow the most ($584 per capita) and spend the most in interest payments to retire the general debt ($42 per capita). On average, metropolitan counties spend more on retiring the debt than they do on providing such services as health, highways, police protection, fire protection, and parks and recreation. Of course, borrowing funds is used to finance capital facilities such as police and fire stations and is part of service delivery costs. Total county debt to finance capital projects and payment of interest to retire debt is growing. Interest payments consume an increasing proportion of revenues. There does not appear to be a slowing down or reversal of this borrowing trend. Most examinations of service delivery do not take into account the increasing demands for borrowing brought on by growth.

As with most observations about counties, there is much variation as to how much of their expenditures is committed to payment of interest on general debt. Although larger counties borrow and pay more interest, state influence, particularly constitutional and statutory limits regulating county debt, plays a significant role in explaining county expenditures for debt service. Florida's metropolitan counties spend the most to retire the debt—at $109 per capita. By contrast, California counties spend about one-fourth as much with an average of $27 per capita (U.S. Bureau of the Census, 1990). Although California and Florida are heavily urbanized, counties in these states differ as to the extent they borrow to finance infrastructure and public facilities. The national average for interest payments of metropolitan counties is $42 per capita. This figure is influenced most by the state in which the county is located. States such as Arizona, Florida, Maryland, Tennessee, and West Virginia allow counties to borrow a great deal. In contrast, counties in Alabama, Georgia, and Illinois commit very little of their budgets to retire debt.

The magnitude in the types and amount of borrowing is increasing as well. The upward trend in expenditures to retire debt is dramatically altering the "service package" of counties in metropolitan areas. Debt service payments and related county borrowing complicates assessments of the quality and quantity of service benefits distributed to county residents. While the servicing of debt comes from current operating budgets, the benefits are spread out over many years. Payment of interest on debt is not just another commitment to service delivery. Major county resources are being committed to repay debt. The role of financing public services through borrowing is important in assessing the service role of the metropolitan counties (R. Thomas, 1991).

METROPOLITAN COUNTY STATUS: BACK TO CONTEXT

Metropolitan status is only one factor in explaining revenue and service commitments and the general role of metropolitan counties. In all cases, metropolitan status needs to be examined along with other factors when examining the role of counties.

County-State Relations: State Rules and Assistance

The state in which a county is located is critical for understanding the functions of metropolitan counties. Many of the services metropolitan counties provide are state services that are "assigned" to them. Often it is not a matter of urbanization or county population size that drives the agenda of services that are provided. Rather, it is often nothing more than state law, state policy, or availability of state fiscal resources.

For example, Fairfax County, Virginia, is assigned the function of education by state law. Educational expenditures account for more than half the expenditures of Fairfax, and for that matter half of the expenditures of all Virginia counties. Maryland, North Carolina, and Tennessee have also assigned the function of education to their counties. Consequently, the counties in these four states are among the highest in expenditures

across the country, largely because they provide public education. Some
states also require counties to perform such functions as public welfare,
public health, hospitals, and corrections, while other states do not mandate
much of any county involvement with the provision of these services. The
assignment of such services makes a difference, often a big difference, in
the expenditures and agendas of county governments.

The place of counties in the state-local government network in most
parts of the country was also largely shaped prior to the explosion of
suburban growth evident after World War II. Fixed patterns of state
revenues to counties in many states is separate from the pressures generated by urbanization and its related problems. It is not uncommon for
nonmetropolitan counties in Midwestern states to spend twice as much per
capita on roads and highways than do metropolitan counties in the same
state.

On average, states provide counties with ten times the revenue provided
by the national government. Approximately 80 percent of counties do not
receive any direct financial assistance from the national government
(J. Thomas, 1987). States transfer revenues to counties in varying
amounts. Virginia and Maryland transfer to counties approximately 40
percent of all local revenues, much of it for education expenditures. By
comparison, Texas counties receive only about 5 percent of their revenue
from the state (U.S. Bureau of the Census, 1990).

Generally, the more services a state expects a county to perform, the
more state revenues will be provided to the counties to supplement local
revenues. For counties in Texas, the 5 percent revenues received from the
state amount to less than $20 per resident. Texas counties, both metropol-
itan and nonmetropolitan, do not assume a large role in providing services
when compared to counties in other states. In sum, state functional
assignment and fiscal involvement of state government are critical factors
to consider when assessing the service role of metropolitan counties.

Charter Home-Rule Status

The extent to which a county has home rule also has an impact on the
activities of metropolitan county governments. As noted earlier, 24 states
have adopted constitutional amendments or passed legislation allowing
counties to adopt charter government status, which allows them an important measure of discretion in offering services, programs, and altering
structures. Although charter status and home-rule powers vary among
states, they always extend to counties the opportunity to augment state
responsibilities and to be more responsive to local needs (Jeffery, Salant,

and Boroshok, 1989). When given the opportunity, however, few counties have adopted charter government (see Chapter 2). Many of the counties in metropolitan areas, 615 out of 738, do not have charters (T. Salant, 1989).

When metropolitan counties adopt charters, states have given them wider latitude to shape their own service agendas in accordance with local needs. Charter status gives counties the means for responding to metropolitan-induced demands. Among metropolitan counties in New York, a state that allows charter government, there are varying commitments to services among counties. Rockland County spends $170 per capita on hospitals, while several other counties do not provide county hospitals at all. Rensselaer County has made a major commitment to community colleges ($210 per capita). Other metropolitan New York counties do not provide community colleges. In California, another home-rule state, the provision of county hospitals is responsive to local demand and is allowed by charter status. While several metropolitan counties in California do not provide hospitals, two California counties have made major budgetary commitments for them. In Louisiana, various metropolitan counties have made service commitments to providing health services, water, and sewers, in contrast to other metropolitan counties that have made small or no commitments to provide these services.

Charter government and home rule for counties is a facilitating factor in the latitude metropolitan counties have in shaping service commitments. Without home rule, counties are largely limited to providing state-assigned or -mandated services. Large population is not a sufficient catalyst for allowing counties to provide a wider variety of services or to increase their commitment to quality service standards.

Local Government Networks

All metropolitan populations are governed by a multiplicity of local units. The role of the counties varies with the responsibilities given to municipalities and special district governments. Counties in Illinois have not assumed many service obligations in contrast to the cities and special districts in that state. Illinois ranks first in the nation with over 6,000 local units of government compared to a national average of 1,620 local units per state. Counties overlay numerous other types of local units including cities, special districts, and townships. There is an average of 65 local units per county area in Illinois. These other local units in Illinois provide many services that are provided by counties in other states. As citizens and interest groups demand new services or increases in existing services, the county may not be the first unit relied on to provide services. In Illinois, county expenditures remain relatively low at $170 per capita, compared to the national level of $475 (U.S. Bureau of the Census, 1990). This low expenditure figure is not from lack of urban problems, rather it reflects commitments of a complex network of local governments, within which the county plays a relatively circumscribed role.

The two Arizona metropolitan counties of Maricopa (Phoenix) and Pima (Tucson) provide further illustration of the issue of local government overlay. Arizona does not allow counties to adopt home-rule charters. Thus, variation in county service commitments and expenditures cannot be attributed to local choices permitted by home rule. Rather, the existence of other jurisdictions within the two counties probably explains county expenditures and service commitments. Maricopa and Pima counties both have large populations, with 2.5 million and 700,000, respectively. If population size and growth were the primary factor influencing county commitment to service delivery, Maricopa would have much greater expenditures than Pima. The reverse is true. Maricopa had a per capital expenditure of $414 in 1987, whereas Pima County's expenditures were $753, or nearly two-thirds larger than Maricopa's.

A major reason for Pima County's greater expenditure and service commitment is because it has few cities that provide services. There are 4 cities in Pima County in comparison to 21 cities in Maricopa. A sizable portion of Pima County residents live in unincorporated areas where the county is the general-purpose local government. In Maricopa, the proportion of residents living in unincorporated areas is smaller than it is in Pima. Also, Maricopa County has five full-service cities with populations over 100,000., These large suburban cities provide many services that Pima residents must turn to the county to receive. The services Pima provides are primarily infrastructure, such as water, sewage, and highway facilities. These facilities are financed by cities in Maricopa.

CONCLUSION

Population continues to shift from the central city to metropolitan counties. Metropolitan counties' response to this shift depends on their governing ability as provided by state law and the relationship they have to other units of government within their jurisdiction. It is clear, however, that metropolitan county governments have become a key unit of government for many of America's citizens, playing a vital role in providing services and equalizing the tax burden among all income groups. At the same time, they face the problems created by the spread of urban population, demands for more services, and the need to build and renovate infrastructure.

The metropolitan status of counties is important in understanding their role. Metropolitan counties offer more services, provide state services at above the legal minimum standards, and respond to local demands. Often they are assuming a greater share of the service burden placed on all local governments. Yet, metropolitan status is only one factor in assessing county activities. The variation among metropolitan counties is too great to be attributed primarily to their size, density, or their place on the urban-suburban continuum. As one examines county governments across the nation, metropolitan status, charter status, and county relationship to other local governmental units also matter. In some instances, states deny counties much latitude in responding to urban residents' demands. Yet metropolitan counties are evolving into more comprehensive, full-service governmental units. They have adapted new roles and redefined old commitments to meet the challenges they face as a result of urbanization. The many "special" circumstances of counties in metropolitan America create an increasing challenge for further inquiry.

NOTE

The authors like to acknowledge the very helpful comments of Dr. Mavis Mann Reeves of the University of Maryland, Dr. Robert Thomas of the University of Houston, and Dr. Paul M. Hirsch of Georgia State University.

1. We define "metropolitan" county using Census Bureau designations. We feel this definition is more descriptive of urban counties than those that use only population because it includes smaller counties whose policy and service delivery activities are affected by encroaching urbanization.

Chapter 7

The Special Problems of Rural County Governments

Beverly A. Cigler

Rural communities play a central role in American life. They have served as the standard-bearers of "grass-roots democracy" and represent the values of community and individualism. Rural areas provided the labor, food, and other natural resources that supported the industrial revolution. The Office of Technology Assessment (OTA) views rural communities as a haven from problems caused by urban development (1991). County government is the most visible and important type of government for most rural residents.

This chapter reviews the diversity of rural America, the problems of rural county governance, and the capacity-building activities directed at rural governments. The chapter concludes with a discussion of expected trends in rural county governance in the 1990s.

RURAL AMERICA

Defining Rural

There are no completely acceptable definitions of what is meant by "urban" or "rural." The differences are found in population density and occupational differences, although variations in social and economic organization and in attitudes and values are involved. Urban and rural are not two clearly defined categories.

The U.S. Census Bureau defines rural as any place of fewer than 2,500 residents. Nationally, 26 percent of the population was rural in this sense as of the 1980 Census. For looking at historical trends since 1900, data are most readily available according to this Census Bureau definition.

Another method in use by federal statistical agencies defines as metropolitan or urban all of those counties that include a total population of at least 50,000, or an urbanized area of at least 50,000 with a total county population of at least 100,000. This definition classifies as rural some areas that have prominent urban characteristics and includes in the urban category very rural portions of those counties classified as urban. Despite these drawbacks, a nonmetropolitan definition of rural has one distinct advantage: because it is based upon county units, it provides the most extensive data available to make contemporary comparisons between rural and urban America.

The economic and social diversity of rural America makes it difficult to present an accurate portrayal of rural counties. Rural used to be synonymous with farming. However, by the 1980s less than one-tenth of rural residents actually farmed, and nonfarm income represented two-thirds of the American farm family's household budget. The Economic Research Service (ERS), the largest federal unit devoted entirely to research on rural issues, uses the Census definition of metropolitan and nonmetropolitan counties and reports most of its data on that basis. ERS developed and uses population codes—called Beale codes after their originator, Calvin Beale—to differentiate between rural and nonrural counties. For each Beale code, Table 7.1 shows the definition, the number of counties in the category, and the 1984 population figure.

Many respected sources consider Beale codes 4 though 9 as nonmetro counties, based on how urban (or rural) their population is and on how close they are to metro areas (P. Salant, 1990, 2). The General Accounting Office (GAO, 1989) recently took a more restrictive definition and treated rural counties as Beale codes 6 though 9. About two-thirds of all U.S. counties are rural under this definition, making ruralness a key factor to consider when examining county government. The more restrictive GAO definitions (those treating Beale codes 4 through 9 as rural) place 24 percent of the U.S. population and 28 percent of its labor force in rural areas (e.g., see Office of Technology Assessment, 1991).

Another refinement that can be made to nonmetropolitan (i.e., rural) county designations is to use the Policy Impact or ERS County-Type coding system (Bender et al., 1985). This identifies seven types of rural counties according to three characteristics: their major economic base, the presence of federally owned land, and population characteristics (including retirement and persistent poverty). The seven rural county types, and the percentage of all rural counties of that type are:

1. Counties heavily dependent on farming, 29 percent
2. Counties heavily dependent on manufacturing, 28 percent
3. Mining-dependent counties with economies based mainly on nonre-
    newable natural resources, 8 percent
4. Counties with high concentrations of government activities and/or
5. Federal lands counties, 13 percent (4&5 combined)
6. Persistent poverty counties, 10 percent
7. Counties characterized as retirement settlements, 20 percent

Some counties do not fit into any category and others can be placed into more than one category, thus, the total exceeds 100 percent.

The diversity of social and economic conditions across the rural counties of the four Census regions—West, Midwest, Northeast, and South—is immense. Persistent poverty counties occur primarily in Appalachia, the Ozark-Ouachita Plateau, and the Mississippi Delta. Retirement counties are usually located in remote rural areas, with large concentrations in eastern Texas, in the Ozarks, in Florida, in parts of the Upper Great Lakes states, and in several Western states. More than half of the manufacturing counties are in the Southeast; others are concentrated in the North-Central region, with still others found in the Northwest and Northeast. These counties tend to be the most urbanized of the nonmetro counties and are more likely to be adjacent to a metropolitan area.

Remote counties, concentrated in the North-Central U.S. and scattered along the Mississippi River Delta, parts of the Southeast, and in Idaho, Montana, and Washington, make up the farming-dependent counties. The coal-producing areas of Appalachia and the Midwest; the oil-producing parts of Texas, Oklahoma, and the Louisiana Gulf Coast; and many parts of the Southwest and West have mining-dependent counties. Specialized government counties are scattered throughout the United States, with federal lands counties in the West (Bender et al., 1985; P. Salant, 1990).

The Rural Economy

The decade of the 1970s produced a unique historical trend: a reversal in the movement of people from rural to urban areas in virtually all regions of the United States. Rural (nonmetropolitan) areas grew faster than urban (metropolitan) areas, and migration from cities exceeded migration to cities. Rural employment grew faster than urban employment and unemployment was generally lower than in urban areas.

Table 7.1
Definitions, Number of Counties, and 1984 Population, by Beale Code

Beale Code	Definition	Number of Counties	Population
0	Central counties of metropolitan areas of 1 million population or more	52	65,548,579
1	Fringe counties of metropolitan areas of 1 million population or more	173	40,074,216
2	Counties in metropolitan areas of 250,000 to 1 million population	289	52,407,144
3	Counties in metropolitan areas of 250,000 population	198	21,821,618
4	Urban population of 20,000 or more, adjacent to a metropolitan area	144	10,862,532
5	Urban population of 20,000 or more, not adjacent to a metropolitan area	143	8,436,239
6	Urban population of less than 20,000, adjacent to a metropolitan area	546	14,720,775
7	Urban population of less than 20,000, not adjacent to a metropolitan area	767	15,730,911
8	Completely rural, adjacent to a metropolitan area	219	2,467,705
9	Completely rural, not adjacent to a metropolitan area	565	4,100,052
Total		3,096	236,169,771

Source: Developed from various Economic Research Service, U.S. Department of Agriculture reports.

Several broad forces are associated with the transition: (1) employment-related factors resulting primarily from technological changes created a new economic base for many communities; (2) the "pull" of an improved quality of life was brought by the ability to offer more and better physical and social services; (3) the "pull" of greater participation in the larger urban society afforded through improved technological linkages (e.g., cable TV) and other cultural influences; (4) the "push" of traditional antiurban attitudes, as well as desires to renew ties to one's area of birth or former residence; and (5) retirement opportunities (Cigler, 1984). Many thought that the so-called rural renaissance would eventually eliminate the disparities between urban wealth and rural poverty.

In the late 1970s, however, the rural economy encountered a downturn. That process intensified in the 1980s as three distinct but coinciding economic difficulties produced severe dislocations in several sectors important to the rural economy (U.S. Department of Agriculture [USDA], 1989; Reeder, 1990):

- The 1981–82 recession affected rural America more than urban America. Cities are more service-oriented and less manufacturing-oriented than previously.

- The farm financial crisis in the mid-1980s was characterized by declines in farmland values, farm income, and population.

- The energy industry slump reached its low point in 1986–87.

Many rural areas today show signs and symptoms that raise concern for their futures. Much economic vitality has been lost. Rural areas have experienced a relative decline in income. High unemployment, low work-force participation, and a high level of out-migration are serious concerns. Rural per capita income—especially in the most rural areas—is much lower than in urban areas. The rural poverty rate—on an upswing since the early 1970s—stands 35 percent higher than the metro rate (U.S. Department of Agriculture, 1988). Between 1980 and 1988, the nonmetropolitan population grew only 4.7 percent, less than half the metro area growth rate. Between 1982 and 1987, almost half of the nonmetropolitan counties lost population, especially those low population counties not in close proximity to a metropolitan area (Braaten, 1991).

The economic events of the 1980s cannot simply be attributed to cyclical trends and other short-term conditions that affect major rural industries. The nonmetro economy has not recovered to its former levels as more normal conditions have been restored in those industries. Overall, the nonmetro recovery has been slow and uneven over the face of a diverse rural America. The forces that underlie the problems that beset rural communities are structural in nature and not easily reversed. The USDA (1989) and Brown and Deavers (1987) list the following structural changes:

- There has been a dramatic shift in the economy away from the production of primary resources and manufactured goods toward the provision of services. Since rural areas are more dependent on these declining sectors, they are especially vulnerable to this shift (U.S. Department of Commerce, 1989). The rural economy itself is slowly shifting from goods to services. Goods production fell from 40 to 35 percent of nonmetro employment between 1979 and 1986; service production rose from 60 to 65 percent (USDA, 1989).

- The emergence of a global economy and the rise of the newly industrialized countries means that rural areas face intense competition in resources and primary manufacturing from abroad. It is more difficult to compete on the basis of low wages with Third World locations that have even lower wage environments.

- The role of natural resources in the rural economy is shifting from resources as raw materials to resources as amenities. This replaces traditional jobs with new ones in recreation-related service industries.

- The rural economy remains specialized in low-wage, low-skill production industries. These offer workers lower pay and less job security than is the case with managerial and technical jobs located in urban areas.

- Labor-saving automation introduced by rural manufacturers has replaced workers in some industries.

- Innovative industries with the best growth potential are concentrated in urban areas. Since 1975 the ratio of more advanced and complex industries, compared to routine production industries, increased over 25 percent in metro areas but was relatively unchanged in nonmetro areas.

- The few high tech firms that have moved into rural areas usually offer low-skill assembly jobs, not the more highly paid scientific or technical positions.

- Rural areas do not compete well with major urban centers in business services, the fastest growing and best paying part of the service sector.

- College-educated and young nonmetro workers are drawn out of rural areas more than three times faster than high school graduates. This is largely due to the 35 percent difference in earning potential between urban and rural workplaces.

A rural area's ability to respond to these macro forces of change, especially industrial restructuring, is greatly limited by being "rural."

Small population size and low-density settlement patterns constrain the ability of rural areas to compete economically with large cities. More than 60 percent of nonmetro counties are not adjacent to a metropolitan area and, thus, receive little benefit from urban growth via commuting or the spillover of economic activity.

The lack of urban amenities, poor job skills, poor school systems (high dropout rates in schools), limited health care systems, and other obstacles hamper the attraction of knowledge-intensive industries that are the leading growth sectors in the national economy. Rural communities are generally lacking in the institutional expertise that could help develop appropriate strategies to meet the challenges that confront them. Most have caretaker governments with few professional managers or planners, and fewer university institutes and other channels for expertise and assistance.

On the other hand, some major changes in U.S. society may offer positive advantages for rural areas. For example, dramatic advances in communication and information technologies and the ways in which such technologies are used can reduce the significance of two factors that disadvantage rural areas: distance and space. In effect, such technologies have a leveling effect among communities (Cigler, 1989).

RURAL COUNTY GOVERNMENTS

Rural local governments are no more homogeneous than are rural economies. Differences in the local institutional structure hamper generalizations about the characteristics of rural county government, impacts of any institutional changes on the structure of local governments, or the needs of a particular county government. In most rural states, counties are the dominant general-purpose local government. Elsewhere, cities and school districts provide most services. In New England and across the northern tier of states, townships may replace both the city and county as the most important general-purpose government, however (Stinson, 1990).

Rural County Roles and Responsibilities

Some contrasts between urban and rural county structure can be made. Rural county governments are most likely to play the role of "administrative arm of the state." Moreover, because many rural counties contain unincorporated areas, rural counties often must provide countywide services. Charter government, the most common type of home rule, has more appeal in urban counties and in areas with constituencies supportive of reform.

Rural counties are governed most usually by boards of commissioners and boards of supervisors with three to five members who serve in both legislative and executive capacities. Most of the rural counties, in addition, independently elect row officers, such as sheriff, attorney, recorder, assessor, and treasurer. These officers have functional authority independent of the governing board (T. Salant, 1989; 1991).

It is difficult to exercise executive leadership when counties are run by a board, with no equivalent of a mayor and with little authority over other independently elected officers. The consensus of government experts is that it makes little sense to elect people whose function often is little more than that of a file clerk. In the case of sheriffs, many question whether the decision as to who should hold office should be based on popularity rather than professional expertise.

Part-Time, Costly Government

Most of rural America relies on part-time and volunteer elected officials who make vital resource decisions daily that affect the availability and quality of services. Often these rural officials have limited or no previous training or experience in making such decisions, as compared to urban areas where decisions are more likely aided by professional planning staff. In addition to the unique structural problems of the rural economy, the relatively low population densities in rural counties, compared to their urban counterparts, pose another problem. In general, the cost per taxpayer of providing public services goes down as population increases. Consequently, rural areas are often unable to afford the same level and quality of public services as urban places. Traditionally, rural residents have demanded fewer services, but that is changing. Yet another reason for costly rural government stems from the sheer number of local government units, which confounds attempts to encourage local cooperation in the delivery of public services.

County Governance Capacity

The 1980s were a time of rethinking the role of rural governments in a changing national economy; such concerns continue into the 1990s. Can smaller, basically unprofessionalized governments perform increased service delivery responsibilities? Can they bring forth the amount of policy coordination necessary for managing a decentralized system, while preserving local autonomy? What are the needed capacity-building efforts for development of local officials' awareness about their roles, as well as enhancement of their abilities to govern? (Cigler, 1984).

Honadle (1981, 1984) defines government capacity as the ability to anticipate and influence change; make informed, intelligent decisions about policy; develop programs to implement policy, attract and absorb resources, manage resources, and evaluate current activities to guide future action. One of the great dilemmas of governance in the United States is the uneven resource base among local governments. Professionalization is associated with larger units of government, but more than 90 percent of the municipal and township governments in the United States service communities of fewer than 10,000. More than 80 percent of U.S. municipalities serve under 5,000 people each. More than 75 percent of county governments serve populations of fewer than 50,000 people. Approximately 67 percent of all governmental units exist in rural areas and have limited management capacity (Cigler, 1989).

The lack of professional management expertise within rural governments is well-recognized (Brown, 1980; Loomis and Beegle, 1975; Lewis, 1986; Sokolow, 1986). Most rural counties do not have a full-time professional manager or administrator skilled in the basic internal management skills—including the control functions of budgeting and personnel systems, or knowledge about specific kinds of service delivery. This is especially problematic in light of the view that technical expertise must be coupled with an understanding of the greater political environment, especially the many interconnections in which all counties now exist.

Rural governments have been hard-hit by decreased federal aid and dwindling budgets, public concern over waste, growing service demand, increasing calls for efficiency and effectiveness in government operations, and unfunded mandates from the states and national government. As the home of most of America's natural resources and open spaces, rural counties experience growing involvement with solid waste management, water quality, and clean air problems. All types of human service issues—affordable housing, AIDS, juvenile justice, cable TV, natural and technological disasters, emergency medical services and hospital care, and such—are part of a rural county's responsibilities.

Whether facing economic decline or rapid growth caused by urban spillover and increased service demands (e.g., former New York City and Philadelphia residents moving to rural northeast and southeast Pennsylvania and commuting to the cities), rural areas must meet local public service needs that are driven by economic forces beyond their immediate control. Rural counties struggle to find new revenues to compensate for the loss of federal financial assistance. New oversight and planning responsibilities must be handled, particularly in the area of environmental planning. Federal and state regulations for water quality, solid and hazardous waste management, and farmland preservation are examples. The growing complexity and increased skills requirements of the economy place a greater premium on providing quality education. With a growing proportion of the population reaching retirement age, additional services for the aging are needed. The demand for public services in rapid growth regions increases at a rate faster than local revenues for providing them. A significant share of rural America's roads, bridges, sewer and water systems must be rebuilt and be better maintained than in the recent past or even more jobs, population, and tax revenues will be lost.

Increased Conflict and Complexity

Just as economic decline poses serious governance challenges for rural county government, rapid growth in some rural counties has dramatic impacts on politics and management. Conflicting community attitudes about growth and the reluctance of residents to support tax increases often result in reactive, not anticipatory, action by rural officials. Traditionally, rural counties are the least likely to have comprehensive land use policies (Cigler, 1979). Coordination difficulties with other governments in the county increase, especially when no professional planning agency or staff are available. Bender and Zolty's research (1986) shows that rapid growth permeates all aspects of a government and community. Decision processes that were once brief, informal, and relatively conflict-free become time-consuming, rule-bound, and often immersed in conflict. Much the same effects result as rural counties experience federal or state funding cuts, unfunded but controversial mandates, and more environmental and social problems.

Fiscal Stress

Suggestions by Loomis and Beegle (1975) and Weinberg (1984) that there are differences between urban and rural governments in retrenchment policy are supported by the empirical examinations of rural municipal and county government fiscal stress of Cigler (1986) and MacManus and Pammer (1990). Cigler's North Carolina study was later replicated by researchers participating in the fiscal stress research conducted by the National Small Government Research Network (e.g., Cigler's 1991b Pennsylvania study). All of the research suggests that rural jurisdictions are likely to cut resources at a higher rate than they seek new revenues, while urban jurisdictions are more likely to turn to a gamut of revenue-raising options. Small governments have fewer revenue options in general. Dependence on the property tax poses problems.

Privatization and Third-Party Government

Another issue of increasing concern for rural counties deals with the movement of government toward privatization in its many forms. Workable third party service delivery arrangements (e.g., contracting with the private sector for solid waste pick-up) require that officials pay increased attention to accountability concerns. Technical skills are needed to ensure that sound contracts are written, for example, and that private contracts are monitored. One investigation of county monitoring of private sector contracts for various types of service delivery found great concern with such issues but little action to meet the accountability challenges (Cigler, 1990).

Federal Aid

An analysis of both urban and rural counties by Rymarowicz and Zimmerman (1988) found that counties experienced a 73 percent decrease in direct federal aid as a percentage of total revenues between 1980 and 1986. Rural areas have been especially hard hit. The slow growth of rural counties has caused a financial gap in property tax collections; the loss of revenue-sharing was especially problematic.

It can be argued that still existing federal aid is unevenly matched to current rural problems. According to a 1989 General Accounting Office report, about 17 percent of federal domestic funding goes directly to rural counties. The percentages of such funding, however, vary widely among various federal agencies. U.S. Department of Agriculture programs have the highest average of program funds going directly to rural counties—50 percent; the Department of Housing and Urban Development programs and Department of Energy programs have the lowest averages—4 percent and less than 2 percent, respectively (GAO, 1989).

Of approximately 800 federal domestic assistance programs, four categories stand out as containing the principal rural development-type programs: (1) economic development (i.e., programs that assist business and industry); (2) agriculture and natural resources (i.e., programs that assist food and fiber producers); (3) infrastructure (i.e., programs that help states, communities, and others construct and maintain community facilities, transportation systems, utilities, and public works); and (4) human resources (i.e., programs that provide education, employment and jobs training, health services, community services, and housing).

The 1989 GAO study identified 88 programs in those four development categories that met the definition of rural development-type programs. The 88 programs provided total funding to both rural and nonrural counties of about $29 billion in fiscal year 1987. Rural share data for fiscal year 1985 were available for 48 of the programs. The 48 programs provided approximately $17 billion, of which about 21 percent went directly to rural counties.

CAPACITY-BUILDING

National Role

The major actor in rural capacity-building at the national level is the U.S. Department of Agriculture, especially its Economic Research Service, Cooperative Extension Service (and the State land-grant colleges and university systems), as well as the Farmers Home Administration (FmHA), and Soil Conservation Service (SCS). The National Governors' Association and several private foundations also play key roles. The various states have an uneven recent history in dealing with their rural areas. Conspicuously absent in most of these efforts, however, is a strong or even visible role for rural county government elected officials.

In recent years, there has been an emphasis on expanding USDA's focus beyond agriculture-related issues to include more general economic development issues affecting rural areas. This was a key recommendation of USDA's Rural Revitalization Task Force report, *A Hard Look at USDA's Rural Development Programs* (1989). Without a major organizational restructuring—and within their current budgetary resources—USDA developed a strategic approach to rural development. The effort attempts to make USDA's programs mutually supportive and refocused on long-term economic development, not just program-specific intermediate objectives.

Title XXIII of the Rural Economic Development Act of 1990 (Public Law 101–624) reorganizes the USDA to play a major leadership and coordinating role by creating the Rural Development Administration. USDA now coordinates rural policy and chairs the interagency committee on rural development that operates under the auspices of the White House Economic Policy Council.

Several initiatives put forth by the Bush administration have lagged in appropriations. However, the key element—the development of State

Rural Development Councils (SRDCs)—became operative in eight pilot states in 1991 (Kansas, Maine, Mississippi, Oregon, South Carolina, South Dakota, Texas, and Washington) and is scheduled for expansion in late 1992. The SRDCs are composed primarily of federal rural development program representatives and members who represent state rural development programs, local government organizations, and private enterprise. Rural counties as units of government, however, do not generally play a significant role in the SRDCs. The functional responsibilities of the SRDCs are:

- to develop better state-level interdepartmental and intergovernmental rural development relations;

- to inventory rural economic development needs in the state and identify alternative solutions for dealing with rural development needs;

- to design a state strategy for applying available resources to achieve long-term rural economic development; and

- to implement, in cooperation with the states, local governments, and the private sector, the state rural economic development strategy. The Rural Economic Development Institute, located at the University of Wisconsin-Madison, conducts training sessions for SRDC members.

The Economic Research Service within USDA is the major research agency on rural areas. FmHA, with offices located in rural counties, offers a variety of loan and grant programs designed to improve the quality of life and to meet the financing needs of rural residents and communities. SCS has a long history of helping farmers; its role has increased as rural issues are increasingly tied to environmental issues.

Another USDA component, the Cooperative Extension Service, has made a major effort to shift more attention and resources to the community development aspects of its mission. Considerable effort, although still quite uneven across the state land-grant institutions, has been devoted to rural economic development, especially leadership training. A great deal of this has been funded by the Kellogg Foundation, which has a sustained interest in rural capacity-building that takes a communitywide partnership focus. Once again, formal participation by elected county officials is not common. Kellogg also funds significant public awareness and action programs on specific issues that affect rural areas, such as groundwater problems.

The National Governors' Association (John, Batie, and Norris, 1988) has done research on rural areas and developed action programs. A noteworthy venture, funded by national foundations in 1990–91, was the selection of ten states to attend a Rural Policy Academy. The program has since continued with the addition of more states. The Academy does training in collaboration with the National Governors' Association, the Corporation for Enterprise Development, the USDA Economic Research Service, and the USDA Extension Service. National experts help teams of state decisionmakers define their rural development problems and opportunities, craft strategic approaches aimed at rural revitalization, and carry out the policies they develop. Participating states develop strategic and comprehensive blueprints, tailored to their unique conditions and priorities, for addressing rural development issues. The Academy places a particular emphasis on efforts to address the needs of economically distressed rural places and people.

State Roles

While there has not been remarkable progress in state government capacity-building for rural areas, there is a growing trend toward such a role. Many governors now have rural advisers. Pennsylvania and New York have rural units created by the legislature. It is commonplace for states to create rural revitalization task forces. Nearly every state has had some strategic planning initiative for economic development, with rural areas included. Rural county governments, however, generally do not play a major formal role in any of these efforts. This may be because of the lack of planning units within such governments.

The basic assumptions that tend to guide state actions are:

- Rather than work toward agreement on a formal definition of "rural" for policy-making and capacity-building assistance purposes, the states are concerned with differences in scale, remoteness, administrative capacity, fiscal capacity, and socioeconomic conditions among all types of municipalities and counties.

- The state role is to provide basic assistance in various areas, expertise and coordination when appropriate, and to serve as a point of contact and information. The state serves as a facilitator for local decisionmaking processes.

- "Solutions" must come from local interest and initiative in identifying issues and concerns and harnessing the energies of the broader community or county, not state government. "Partnerships" and cooperative ventures are encouraged; top-down approaches are avoided.

- Without the monitoring of financial, social, and other conditions, as well as some financial assistance, it is assumed that the rural condition will worsen. That is, the states are taking a lead role in making better use of information available on trends, issues, problems, and opportunities for rural areas.

- A more coordinated and comprehensive approach by state agencies themselves is considered necessary for assisting local officials. Much of what is emerging in state capacity-building is treated in the next section of this chapter, which reports on trends affecting rural county governments.

TRENDS AFFECTING RURAL COUNTY GOVERNMENTS

Service Delivery Cooperation

It may be that the problems of rural America are driving increased efforts at cooperation, coordination, and collaboration at the local level. Counties in most states have made a marked effort in joint ventures with their municipalities. Such cooperation occurs in rural counties primarily in solid waste but also in the general areas of criminal justice policies. There are some recent consolidations in rural areas that have been facilitated by state action. In Montana, the state's new constitution (1972) gave local government the opportunity to consolidate. Two cities and counties, Anaconda and Deer Lodge County, and Butte and Silver Bow County, consolidated in order to conserve resources and manage services more efficiently. At the time, they were faltering economically due to a floundering mining industry.

Formal consolidation of governments may never be widespread. There is a trend, however, toward functional consolidations in specific policy areas. Often, this means that a rural county will assume service delivery for several municipalities, such as a regional police force.

Several states have circuit-rider or "roving public administrator" programs (e.g., Pennsylvania and Georgia, respectively)—often with state funding—to encourage local governmental cooperation. Professional administrators are shared by several counties, for example. Some states have developed an incentive structure to promote service delivery cooperation. More points can be offered for grant applications that include multicounty cooperation or formal cooperation between a county and its municipalities.

Self-Help Strategies

Some rural counties are actively involved in self-development strategies to generate local jobs or income. These include such activities as (Flora et al., 1991):

- county-based development programs, organized in conjunction with one or more counties (e.g., agricultural marketing organizations and school-based enterprises);

- local business and industrial development programs (e.g., business incubators, retention and expansion programs);

- tourism and historical development (recreation development, festivals, crafts fairs, downtown revitalization).

The State of Iowa fosters "community clustering" at the regional level. This promotes multicommunity collaboration, including municipalities and counties, largely for economic development. Other states promote regional tax-base sharing options that are not top-down. Some rural counties in Ohio are participating in a tax-base sharing plan that uses an incentive (i.e., economic funds from the county for participating munici-palities) to promote tax-base sharing among municipalities.

Increased State Government Attention to Capacity-Building

The Georgia State Legislature recently passed legislation that requires local elected officials to complete local government training courses. Aided by university training specialists at the University of Georgia, elected rural officials have access to considerable expertise about their expansive job responsibilities. Although no penalties are imposed for failure to participate in the training programs, officials hoping to be reelected presumably will complete the training. Georgia's program may stimulate a trend; several other states are considering required training and/or certification for various county officials. Fewer training programs exist for elected county officials, however, than for municipal officials.

There is also increased state government interest in building the capacity of those who advise rural government officials. As noted earlier, most rural county governments have part-time, volunteer elected officials at the helm and no professional county managers. Those same officials, however, have access to professionals such as attorneys and financial managers. Research in Pennsylvania revealed the important, if not pervasive, roles played by municipal and county solicitors/attorneys in small, rural governments (Cigler, 1991b). The state's Department of Community Affairs is, thus, developing a handbook for county and municipal attorneys, as well as seminars, in cooperation with the attorneys' professional association. As mandates, finances, and other concerns become more complex, it is difficult for county government advisers to stay abreast of developments in the field.

Capacity-building is not limited to elected officials and their advisers. In most states, community development and organizational capacity-building take on very broad meaning. Leadership development efforts are being expanded to include local and regional utilities and their associations, banking associations, human services groups, and so on. Well-trained and -educated leadership means that both targeted programs (e.g., schools for newly elected officials or specialized curricula for health care, housing, elderly issues) and communitywide leadership development are necessary.

County Reorganization

Plagued by fragmentation, the structures of rural county government often require reorganization and reform in order to meet new challenges effectively. Part of the problem is the great number of semiindependent boards, agencies, and commissions that were created to carry out specialized functions by county governments that were or are constitutionally powerless to provide for themselves. Even in the relatively few home-rule counties, little has been done to coordinate the programs. Given the unlikely ability of rural governments to manage with archaic structures, there will be continuing interest in reorganization. Each year, each state county lobbying association promotes numerous legislative changes that affect the authority of counties within the state, making slow progress.

Revenue Diversification

Related to county reorganization is the general issue of public finance. Some strides have been made in recent years in dealing with unfunded state mandates. A major issue for most states is the local reliance on the property tax and the need for counties to diversify their revenue sources. As the U.S. population ages, the asset-rich (paid-for homes) but cash-poor (must pay property taxes) dilemma looms greater. In the restricted sense, revenue diversification refers simply to the adoption of sales and income taxes (Stinson, 1990). In the broadest sense, revenue diversification can mean many ways to provide high-quality public services at affordable costs via revenue enhancement.

Promoting energy management as a cost-saving tool and exploring alternative service delivery mechanisms are revenue diversifications also.

It is unlikely that many rural areas will die or disappear. Even in areas that do not grow in population, financial problems are not self-correcting. Rural counties must change simply to meet their basic service needs. Population decline may heighten financial problems. Consolidation, inter-local cooperation, contracting, and shared services are all types of revenue enhancement. Building the financial management capacity of small, rural governments emerges as a major concern for the 1990s.

Strategic Vision

Despite the lack of planning agencies within rural county government, there is an overriding need for public policies for growth management, infrastructure, economic development, and environmental concerns. Once again, most rural governments do not have the management or fiscal capacity to make linkages in their policy development and implementation processes. States are beginning to stay abreast of what other states are doing. To economize, they are creating demonstration or pilot projects, focusing on information dissemination of "best practices," and fostering communitywide or countywide partnerships.

CONCLUSION

This chapter depicted rural diversity by examining various definitions of rural and the classifications of rural counties. Historical changes in rural America—especially the effects of macro-economic trends in recent decades—were used to examine whether current rural problems are cyclical or the result of structural economic change. The fragmentation, diversity, and economic problems of contemporary rural America were examined in light of the fact that the predominant government in rural areas is the county. The rural county was depicted as a largely archaic structure, ill-equipped to deal with contemporary problems of governance. Much of the chapter, then, was devoted to an examination of the capacity-building activities of state governments and recent trends in state rural development policy.

NOTE

This chapter was made possible in part by a grant from the Center for Rural Pennsylvania, a Legislative Agency of the Pennsylvania General Assembly.

Chapter 8

Shifting Roles in County-State Relations

Tanis J. Salant

Most counties were created as subunits of states for the purposes of delivering traditional statewide services such as tax assessing and collecting, and to enable sparsely scattered citizens access to government no more than a day's round-trip buggy ride away. The origins of county government were rooted in an agrarian society that needed few governmental services, a low-budget operation with a limited mission. Since midcentury, rural and urban counties alike generally have been evolving into comparatively sophisticated and essential units of government, yet the approach of states toward county government remains rooted in these humble beginnings.

For intergovernmental purposes, the nature and scope of county government have changed almost unimaginably since county boundaries were initially carved. Academics and the media have begun to take notice, particularly with respect to trends in regionalization and devolution of federal programs, but state legislatures, high courts, and administrative agencies often seem to disregard such transformation when addressing county issues.

Counties perform an increasingly vital role as subunits of the state and as local and regional governments, and their fate is played out compellingly in state capitols year after year. The relationship of counties to states is pivotal in how this unit of government functions. Little has been explored on the relationship between counties and states other than to describe constitutional and statutory delineations of authority. Moreover, general discussions of state-local relations have tended to omit references to county government, and studies typically view intergovernmental matters from the top down. This chapter undertakes to investigate contemporary relations between counties and states from the point of view of counties.

The following discussion is based in large part on the results of interviews with officials representing associations of counties. All states—except Connecticut, Rhode Island, and Vermont—have county associations or something similar. The major activities of associations include lobbying the state legislature; interfacing with the executive branch, providing services to county officials such as training, information, and insurance pools; and facilitating the lobbying efforts of county officials (Cigler, 1991a, 5). The executive directors of county associations serve as the principal lobbyists and are generally in the best position to understand a broad array of county issues and concerns.

The survey was conducted by telephone during the months of July and August 1991, after legislative sessions (except that of Massachusetts) had concluded. Responses represent all county associations, and in all cases but two, the executive directors were interviewed. The survey had several questions relating to county interactions and outcomes with the legislature, governor, state agencies, and state courts. After discussing relationships with state institutions, we look at the political influence of counties in state politics and shifts in the balance of power.

STATE LEGISLATURES

View of the Legislature

The relationship between counties and legislatures has traditionally been characterized as contentious and demeaning by county officials, who are often seen (and fostered) by legislators as "grown men groveling with hats in hand" (T. Salant, 1989). But before the one-person one-vote series of rulings in the mid-1960s, at least one house in legislatures tended to be more representative of rural areas, whose members would share a kindred spirit with rural counties. Since the legislative reapportionment of the 1960s, rural interests have lost representation, and counties are now finding urban lawmakers less understanding and sympathetic. Recent studies of the attitudes of elected county officials toward the state confirm growing distrust of the *intent* of states in dealing with counties, particularly with regard to state reticence in providing adequate funding for new or expanded programs (Waugh, 1988; Waugh and Streib, 1989; Streib and Waugh, 1990).

The survey responses in the summer of 1991 reported here reveal similar trends. County association leaders were asked:

1. Describe the relationship between counties in your state and the legislature.
2. Describe the relationship between county officials and their delegations.
3. Does the legislature treat county government like a special interest group or more as a valued partner in governing the state?

Somewhat surprisingly, in light of historically contentious county-legislative relations and the present state fiscal crisis, the majority of executive directors gave favorable assessments. Relations with the legislature were rated "good-to-excellent" by 64 percent (30 states). Relations between elected county officials and their legislative delegations were viewed even more positively, with 70 percent (33 states) in the good-to-excellent range. Some association leaders view this type of interaction their most effective tool and others wish that it would occur on a more regular basis. Table 8.1 arrays responses to the first two questions about the legislature.

Most respondents to the first question, "Describe the relationship between counties in your state and the legislature," offered explanations for their description. Explanations for both positive and negative views seem loosely based on five broad conditions: long-held or changing conceptualizations of county government, legislative outcomes, the makeup of the legislature, the process of interaction (i.e., hard work on the part of county representatives to establish and maintain cooperation and accessibility), and "context" (e.g., prevailing economic conditions).

Positive View

Some of the positively viewed relationships were based on mutual trust and respect, where counties perceived themselves as important; this assessment focuses on legislative attitude rather than on policy outcomes.

Table 8.1
County-Legislative Relations (N = 47)

	Excellent	Good	Fair	Poor	Mixed
Legislature	6/13%	24/51%	7/15%	10/21%	0
Delegation	7/15%	26/56%	8/17%	3/6%	3/6%

Comments included: "We are recognized as important and given a lot of input," and "Our relationship is good because counties have become more credible, but it has been a long process to reach this stage." Good treatment, however, is sometimes due to political expediency; often the political support of elected county officials back home is deemed critical to reelection. Moreover, a positive legislative view of counties has not necessarily been translated into successful outcomes. Suggests one respondent, "Our relationship is cooperative and the legislature is accessible, but ultimately we are not a high priority."

Many positive relations were clearly due to successful legislative outcomes; some described them as: "We got five out of six priorities"; or "We have a good success rate; we got 4 major things and 12 minor things this session." A few positive views were hinged on simply not losing ground during the session: "The relationship is good in that the legislature didn't try to balance the state budget on our backs, but it still views us as a child bottom-line." Others attributed a good relationship to hard work on the part of counties: "Ours is excellent because we work very hard and concentrate on the leadership." But more typically, explanations depict a relationship that exists on two levels: good on the interaction level but poor in actual outcomes. Two responses capture this condition: "It is cooperative with moments of stress; everyone is accessible, but declining state revenues are causing the legislature to shift costs to counties"; and "Legislators are fine in the coffee shop back home, but when they get to the capitol, they clearly work for the state."

While the relationship between counties and the legislature in many states is viewed as generally cooperative, the present state fiscal stress has led to deteriorating relations, chiefly because of the propensity of legislatures to shift costs to counties in bad times. What had been a good—and sometimes outstanding—relationship before 1991 has soured for many. This type of explanation falls into the "contextual" category. Observes one executive director: "Until this year we had a caretaker relationship, but with declining state revenues, a governor who declared 'No new taxes,' and big promises to fund education, courts and corrections, the legislature is now taking general fund monies from counties."

Negative View

The vast majority of responses to explain a poor relationship with the legislature fall into the conceptualization category. Key descriptives include "paternalistic"; lack of trust, respect, appreciation, credibility, or understanding; and "ill-begotten stepchildren." The end result of legislative attitudes tends to be manifested in insufficient authority for counties, expressed as "They don't give us the tools to do our job" or "They've set counties adrift." Other explanations allude to the tone of interaction—tense, adversarial, "every man for himself," or insincere—and point to the increasing practice of shifting costs to counties as the outcome of tensions. Last, several executive directors pinpoint the loss of rural representation in the legislature as the cause of a poor relationship, for "urban legislators have a poorer view of counties."

Delegative Relations

The second question referring to county-legislative relations asked executive directors to describe the relationship between county officials and their legislative delegation. All states affirm that county elected officials do interact with and lobby legislators, with 70 percent reporting a good-to-excellent relationship, 6 percent giving it mixed reviews, and 23 percent claiming it as fair-to-poor. Responses to this question were included in Table 8.1. Most view this aspect of interaction as effective and in some cases the deciding factor in obtaining beneficial legislation. Few problems are encountered; they include difficulty in coordinating a multitude of lobbying efforts, a lack of skills, or a poor rapport with urban legislators.

Legislative Treatment

The third question, "Does the legislature treat county government like a special interest group or more as a valued partner in governing the state?" (NCSL, 1989) was intended to capture the process of interacting with and lobbying the legislature as an institution, regardless of policy outcomes. Some 34 percent (16 states) perceive counties to be treated like a special interest group (SIG), and 11 percent (5 states) feel they are treated as a valued partner; 19 percent (9 states) indicate their treatment is in between, with an additional 15 percent (7 states) on the interest group side of the spectrum and 15 percent on the partner side; 6 percent (3 states) say their treatment depends on the issue or the legislator and cannot be generalized. Table 8.2 displays the spectrum of responses.

Several association directors feel their counties are treated by the legislature no differently than a "tavern association" or "tobacco lobby." In this view, because counties hold no other significance, they are objects to be used. Expresses one respondent, "[Counties] are like a vessel to fill up with additional responsibilities, a place to dump [state programs]." And

Table 8.2
Legislative Treatment (N = 47)

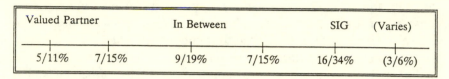

Valued Partner		In Between		SIG	(Varies)
5/11%	7/15%	9/19%	7/15%	16/34%	(3/6%)

as a special interest group, remarks another, "Counties are a loud noisy pain in the butt, and, like the abortion issue, [the legislature] would just like us to go away." In several states, however, county government is seen as moving away from special interest toward partnership, in part because the legislature recognizes that "the state can't get anything done without our support and they have to deal with us."

Legislative Outcomes

Respondents' perceptions of how legislators and legislatures treat counties, particularly in a lobbying capacity, are often not related to their perceptions of legislative outcomes. Many indicate that in spite of a superior or disinterested demeanor on the part of legislators, outcomes of the 1991 legislative session were nonetheless better than expected. Conversely, many who report good treatment by the legislature also acknowledge unfavorable outcomes. Explains one respondent:

> We are well received and they pay a lot of attention to what we say in testimony, but recognition is one thing and policy decisions are another. When pressed, the legislature finds the path of least resistance, which is not to raise state taxes but to let the locals do it.

As one indication of outcomes in the legislature that impact county government, an attempt was made to measure changes in levels of authority for counties. Respondents were asked to identify trends in authority levels since 1985 in fiscal, structural, and functional/ordinance domains (most of which are statutory). A matrix of responses is presented in Table 8.3.

Counties in 31 states gained some authority in at least one domain, with 28 of them reporting fiscal successes. For example, a local option sales tax was authorized in eight states. Other victories include development impact fees; occupational, utility, gas, restaurant, vehicle license, and income taxes; user fees; and a variety of surcharges. The fewest changes

Table 8.3
Changes in Authority Levels (N = 47)

	Fiscal	Structural	Functional
Greater	28/60%	12/26%	10/21%
Same	17/36%	33/70%	37/79%
Less	2/4%	2/4%	0

came in the functional-ordinance area. Only three states report losses in authority, which occurred in additional budget restraints or reduced severance taxes. It should be noted that in many states where authority levels remained unchanged, either changes were not sought or authority was already broad. For example, 2 states already permit broad taxing powers, 11 give wide latitude in the structural area, and 8 convey extensive regulatory powers (Jeffery, Salant, and Boroshok, 1989).

A study conducted by the National Association of Counties (1991) also reports notable gains in the fiscal area for counties during the 1988 and 1989 legislative sessions. Out of 47 county associations 38 responded to a survey seeking legislative outcomes in the domains of taxing authority, mandate relief, and establishing state Advisory Commissions on Intergovernmental Relations. Some 71 percent of respondents (25 states) reported gaining some type of fiscal relief, 20 percent (7 states) gained some type of mandate relief, and 11 percent (4 states) progressed toward establishing a state ACIR. Fiscal relief came principally in the form of new taxing powers, especially for general fund purposes and those dedicated to corrections, roads, and transportation projects. Elimination of or more flexible revenue caps, greater bonding capabilities, and a larger portion of shared revenues were also common.

Findings of both surveys suggest that the vast majority of states (legislatures) are granting new powers to counties, expanding old ones, or extending some kind of relief in fiscal matters. It should be noted, however, that in many cases local referenda are required, which are difficult to pass, or trade-offs are extracted (i.e., counties can now raise the money to pay for state programs), either of which can diminish or negate the gains.

THE GOVERNORS

Governors constitute an important part of county-state relations, although they have less direct impact than legislatures. Governors can help or hinder counties through budget recommendations and use of the veto; they also influence interactions through the opportunity to appoint agency directors, local government liaisons, and establish departments of community affairs or state ACIRs, in which communication, understanding, and negotiation can be facilitated. Additionally, several current governors have previously served in county government, which executive directors claim is a positive influence on relations with the executive branch, if not in policy outcomes. Furthermore, trends in shifting federal programs to the states, while placing strains on state budgets, also can strengthen the office, particularly when the executive branch acts decisively to gain control of federal programs (Hall and Eribes, 1985). The office of governor has gained the *potential* for considerable influence in county affairs.

Association directors were asked to describe the relationship of county government to the governor. Their responses were clearly favorable, as indicated in Table 8.4: 58 percent (27 states) place the relationship in the good-to-excellent range; 38 percent (18 states) rank it fair-to-poor, and 4 percent (2 states) indicate that the relationship had not yet developed enough for assessment (several governors took office in January 1991).

The most favorable assessments, from "extraordinary" to "excellent," are attributed to the governor's establishing good institutional mechanisms to foster intergovernmental cooperation and to appointing good staff as liaisons or agency directors. The negative assessments stem from damaging policy positions or outcomes, lack of understanding or genuine interest in the face of "sympathetic rhetoric," and reneging on promises.

STATE AGENCIES

Interactions with state agencies encompass the functional arena of county-state relations. State agency personnel in program areas (e.g., transportation, health, revenue, environmental quality) supervise the work of bureaucrats in corresponding county agencies (many of whom are elected countywide). This juncture in county-state relations is important because agencies possess substantial quasilegislative and/or judicial powers, often exceeding the "limits of ministerial and managerial tasks" of

Table 8.4
County-Gubernatorial Relations (N = 47)

Excellent	Good	Fair	Poor	(Unknown)
12/26%	15/32%	6/12%	12/26%	(2/4%)

public administration to such a degree that agencies constitute a "fourth branch of government" (Mason and Hink, 1982). It is difficult to measure the degree to which state agencies impact county government, but it is apparent that agency discretion results in additional state power over counties. One analysis concludes:

> To put it simply, state agency personnel may interpret a policy differently than local agency personnel (and both interpretations may be different from that of the state legislature and/or governor). These differences may be minor and go unnoticed. Or they may mean that state and local personnel fight like cats and dogs, simply because they see things differently. Public policy is often determined by the "bureaucratic winners" in these policy battles between local and state agencies (Hamilton and Wells, 1990, 129).

Moreover, certain fiscal and political events have increased the role of both the governor and the administrative wing in many states. Revenue and expenditure limits and other tax reforms require large increases in state expenditures for programmatic areas, notably education and indigent health care, each with commensurate losses in local control. Further, the current state fiscal crises and ensuing cuts in agency budgets have catalyzed agencies into squeezing counties more. One of the most irritating actions is the refusal of state departments of corrections to reimburse counties for housing state felons, even when mandated by the state high court.

Findings from an earlier survey on state agency involvement with local governments indicate that interaction between local and state administrators is frequent, broad, and deep (Wright, 1988, 327). Some 20 to 30 percent of state administrators reportedly had daily or weekly contact with local officials, ranging from reports and inspections to issuing orders. State agencies use an arsenal of tools to aid in supervision, such as persuasion, education, and other noncoercive techniques. "Heavy-handed bureaucrats" appear only when they perceive "incompetence, irresponsibility, or corruption on the part of local bureaucrats" (Adrian, 1967, 101). The biggest irritant in county-state agency relations, however, is the agency practice of handing down administrative mandates by setting policy and changing rules and regulations unilaterally. Observes one researcher on administrative mandates, "They appear very innocuous, but their cumulative impact is enormous (Sylvester, 1989, 29).

The assessments of county officials of the relationship with state agencies are the most difficult to generalize. The tenor of interaction varies from state to state, agency to agency, and between levels of personnel within agencies. Survey responses of executive directors confirm that agencies have impact on counties, and affirm the position of Deil Wright (1988, 333) that "administrative officials are central if not crucial actors in shaping the conflicts, convergence, and compromises evident in the state-local arena."

Executive directors were asked to "describe the relationship of counties to state agencies." The results were less positive than anticipated: 59 percent (28 states) of the respondents ranked the relationship in the good-to-excellent range; 26 percent (12 states) rated it fair-to-poor, and 15 percent (7 states) gave it mixed reviews. Table 8.5 presents responses.

Explanations for having a positive relationship include a good understanding on the part of agency personnel of the environment in which counties operate; good access and room for negotiation; and institutional mechanisms that facilitate communication, such as local government committees within agencies, regular monthly meetings, or joint computer projects. Additionally, relationships with service-type agencies, such as the department of revenue, are generally better than with regulatory ones. Interestingly, relations can be good with one level of an agency (e.g., director or middle management level) while poor with the other.

Problematic relationships surface more in regulatory agencies. Also, normally amicable relations have worsened under recent changes, such as tighter resources, replacement of a director, or a new rule or regulation. As one executive director explains, "Our agencies are cooperative as long as counties comply, but if we try to get any regulations changed, they stonewall." At the worst, laments one respondent, "Regulatory agencies have a 'siege' mentality and counties are the enemy."

STATE COURTS

State courts have an impact on county government as well. County governing boards are familiar with court-issued writs of mandamus occasionally requiring unbudgeted general fund expenditures. The onerous power of judicial mandamus can be mitigated, however, through negotiation and diplomacy at the local level. State high courts have tremendous potential to impact counties on a broader level, particularly in the area of

Table 8.5
County-Agency Relations (N = 47)

Excellent	Good	Fair	Poor	(Varies)
7/15%	21/44%	8/17%	4/9%	(7/15%)

discretionary authority vis a vis state authority (T. Salant, 1988b, 97), but the opportunity for negotiation is less. Zimmerman (1983, Ch. 2) notes that state courts have traditionally interpreted local government powers narrowly, and the tendency for narrow judicial rulings has even served as a disincentive to counties for adopting home rule charters, as discussed later. Furthermore, state courts are having increasingly greater impact in other policy areas, such as local budgeting, development, planning, and housing (Berman, 1989).

To develop a general sense of trends in state court rulings that impact county government, executive directors were asked if there had been recent rulings that have affected counties "to any significant degree." Just over half (26 states) affirm the recent impact of state court decisions. Of this group, 38 percent (10 states) have been impacted favorably, 38 percent (10 states) negatively, and 23 percent (6 states) report mixed results (on two or more rulings) or are uncertain of the resulting impact; 36 percent of all respondents (17 states) report no impact and 2 percent (1 state) were uncertain of the outcome of rulings. Table 8.6 presents responses.

It appears that courts have had recent impacts in half the states, and the impact is equally positive or negative. Courts seem to have broadened their traditionally restrictive views on local powers, particularly with respect to fiscal powers. Funding issues dominate court decisions. The apparent judicial willingness to interpret law in favor of local discretion more than in the past may be due to a generally greater understanding of county government because of the "education" that has occurred from the exercise of county home-rule powers. Another reason may be the increased willingness on the part of counties to challenge rulings. In one state an executive director reports: "Counties are now taking a selectively aggressive attitude in the courts. We challenged a ruling by the state department of health that affected county nursing homes and cost counties $27 million. The court ruled that the department was overstepping its bounds of authority."

The most common explanation for court interference is the trend of courts to shape policy. Offers one executive director, "The Supreme Court

Table 8.6
Consequential Judicial Rulings (N = 44)

Yes (26/59%)			No	Pending
Positive	Negative	Both	17/39%	1/2%
10/38.5%	10/38.5%	6/23%		

is becoming active and trying to shape policy, so the legislature is safer for us now."

COUNTIES: A FRAGMENTED POLITICAL VOICE

Counties have been described as "an overly elected body of government with a ministerial function." They still elect department heads that were created in original state constitutions, allegedly resulting in the ("antiquated") plural executive form of government (or, as some have said, a "headless wonder"). Trimming the "long ballot" by eliminating constitutional officers has been the goal of efficiency experts since the Progressive Era. But what is the bane of reformers could also be the benefit of counties in dealing with the state. Constitutional officers are elected countywide and have a broader political base than members of governing boards, who are usually elected by district. Moreover, unlike many municipal leaders, most county officials are still elected on the basis of party. Many if not most county politicians, who share the same constituency with state legislators, have a stronger political base than their delegation. Few elected officials are more valued by residents than sheriffs and attorneys.

The potential for leverage with the state is vast. County officials have the power to influence legislators, educate state officials on a consistent basis, negotiate with agencies over proposed rule changes, and discuss with the judiciary interpretations or pending rulings that impact county government. In short, county officials operate from a considerable power base and state legislators, who are generally less well known in their district, often seek the support of county officials. (High-level appointed professionals have the potential to build power bases as well.)

The support of local politicians is also one incentive for legislators to draft special legislation that benefits single counties. Sometimes called "going home bills," they can be an appropriation for a road project, a one-time fiscal bailout, a temporary county sales tax for a specific purpose. The legislator gets the credit, but the county gets relief. And if education, diplomacy, and negotiation do not work, county officials also have the option of aggressively challenging state actions in court, as several states are discovering. As suggested earlier, state high courts are moving away from their habit of interpreting local powers narrowly.

Two factors that became evident as interviews progressed were the timidity of county officials in using their political influence and an obliviousness to the impact that a unified county voice could produce. One respondent states directly that "There is no question that commissioners could flex their political muscles with the legislature, but they are not brave." And another articulates a remedy: "Counties are reluctant to challenge [state agency] decrees; rather, they just scramble to figure out how to comply. . . . They need to develop self-confidence, capacity, and a mechanism to help them become proactive."

Some counties are beginning to discover their potential. "When the sheriffs show up in uniform to testify with county commissioners, it makes a difference because they do have power," describes one respondent. Another comments that "our county officials are coming to realize that they have clout, especially when they speak with one voice." As an example of a unified proactive approach, one executive director relays this success: "We introduced and got passed a bill that mandates that state agencies contemplating a new computer system must go through a special review board that includes us. This has helped a great deal to curb their power over us."

Ambivalence or timidity on the part of county officials is evident in operations as well. Executive directors in 40 states (85 percent) say their counties need more authority, especially in the fiscal domain. Only 8 (17 percent) indicate no additional authority is needed, "just more resources." Yet 33 executive directors also report that county officials in their state do not use all of the authority they have. In a few cases, authority is not used because either the resources are lacking or it is not needed, but the majority are unwilling to exercise all their authority for reasons that likely have bearing on state perceptions of county government.

Some respondents point to a "dark ages mentality" among county governing board members, those presumably in more rural areas who have not recognized the changes that have occurred in county government. This approach to governing typifies an unwillingness to use authority when called for. One executive director articulates it this way: "County officials are not comfortable with exercising their authority. We urge them to try doing new things. We have perception problems inhouse, too, from those who view counties as limited rural governments and haven't accepted the changes."

Another approach typifies those who want to do things but will not initiate without legislative permission. One respondent describes: "We have a statute that permits counties to do anything that is not prohibited; it couldn't be broader, the sky's the limit. But commissioners still go to the legislature to get permission when they don't need to. . . . Commissioners weren't ready for all the authority they got at the time."

Still another approach stems from a reluctance to initiate unless forced to do so, presumably to avoid political consequences of decisions, a "make us do it" attitude. Comments another, "We want money and authority, but when problems get sticky, it's the state's responsibility." Some legislatures even accuse counties of "not biting the bullet," and embark on passing new legislation to facilitate their exercise of power. One recent study on actual versus perceived county discretionary authority concludes that county officials underestimate the authority they have (Martin, 1991).

County officials have long resented being treated as ill-begotten step-children made to grovel with hat in hand, but seeking permission when they already have it likely reinforces legislative paternalism. A state legislator explains: "Their subservient behavior feeds our paternalism, and county officials submit to this treatment because they are reticent to stand up to the state for fear of punishment" (T. Salant, 1989, 40).

SHIFTS IN THE BALANCE OF POWER

Though states maintain ultimate authority over county governments, counties have been whittling away at state supremacy and asserting themselves through a variety of strategies and institutional arrangements. As we progress through the 1990s, the potential for shifting the balance of power meaningfully has never been greater.

As counties seek creative ways to finance and deliver ever-expanding services, they are steadily gaining statutory authority from states and rearranging old frameworks, especially in the finance domain where it is most needed. State courts are also appearing more amenable to upholding greater levels of authority, particularly as counties seek redress from unreasonable state dominance.

An interest among counties in home rule and charter adoption persists; increasing numbers of state ACIRs and departments of community affairs provide counties with greater visibility and control; and legislation to mitigate against unfunded mandates is catching on. It appears, as one observer discerns, that "the winds of change are beginning to pick up force in state capitols around the country . . . [though] we still seem to be in the early stage of a major long-term shift. . . . We've raised the level of consciousness about state-local issues" (Gold, 1988).

The old subserviency model of county-state relations appears outdated. While states may seem to view counties as servants or special interest bodies, recent trends in legislation suggest that behavior and policy outcomes might be two different things. Actual legislative outcomes suggest a relationship tending toward the partner side. Whether the begin-ning stage of this "major long-term shift" reaches the next phase is largely up to the initiative of counties. The state fiscal crisis coupled with the predominance of county government in delivering regional services have created an opportunity for counties to propel such a shift.

This encouraging development in county-state relations is tempered, however, by the concomitant trend in state mandating without funds, a practice that can make illusory any real gains in fiscal powers by allowing counties to raise taxes so that states do not have to. Another observer notes:

> For many local officials, budget problems are being compounded by state policies. States with deficit problems are cutting aid to localities or to programs they help localities to fund. . . . States have also been more willing this year to balance their own budgets at local expense, raising additional revenues by finding new things to make localities pay for (Herbers, 1990).

This development calls for a strategy on the part of counties to fight unfunded mandates aggressively in the courts. Counties in one state initiated and spearheaded a referendum to prohibit new unfunded mandates, where the local media depicted county government hitting the legislature in the head with a baseball bat. It passed with 75 percent of the vote.

Chapter 9

Counties and the
National Agenda

David R. Berman and Barbara P. Greene

Counties and other local governments exist in law simply as the creatures of their states. This legal status, however, has not prevented the establishment of direct ties between local governments and the national (federal) government. Indeed, such ties have deep roots in the history of the nation (Hamilton and Wells, 1990, 173; Nice, 1987, 161). During the depression years of the 1930s and again in the 1960s and early 1970s, these relations intensified with the creation of several programs calling for cooperation among the federal, state, and local governments in combating various problems.

As the federal government became more involved in domestic policy, it used state governments to administer many of the programs it financed. The states, in turn, called on their administrative arms, in many instances the county, to provide the function or service funded at the federal level. County and other local officials welcomed the additional funds coming from the national government, though they were not always enthusiastic about how the money was distributed or by the conditions placed on its use (Torrence, 1974, 173).

National associations representing state and local officials have encouraged the growth of the federal role in funding domestic programs. These associations commonly describe themselves as "public interest groups" (PIGs). Together they form the "intergovernmental lobby" (Beer, 1977). Currently among the intergovernmental public interest groups that keep an eye on developments in Washington and try to shape them are the National League of Cities, the National Association of Towns and Townships, the United States Conference of Mayors, the National Governors' Association, and the National Association of Counties.

The influence of these intergovernmental groups has varied over the years. Many of the older organizations helped spur the rapid expansion of the federal role in domestic policy in the depression years of the 1930s. The 1950s brought hard times for them, as the federal government generally scaled down its activities. The 1960s and early 1970s found the organizations involved once again in a flurry of federal activity. They were particularly instrumental in bringing a shift in federal funding from categorical grants to less restrictive block grants (Haider, 1974). Since the late 1970s, however, the state and local lobbies in Washington have met more difficult barriers and, to some extent, have been forced to rethink their roles (Walters, 1991).

In the contemporary era of "new federalism" or "fend-for-yourself" federalism, the lobbying activities of local officials at the state level are far more important than they are at the federal level. As former NACo executive director, John Thomas, recently noted: "County governments live and die at the state legislature. What Congress does to us is irrelevant in many ways" (Walters, 1991, 35). Nevertheless, counties and other local governments continue to have much at stake in Washington, if nothing more than to ward off further cuts and mandates. In this chapter we look into the national agenda of counties as represented in the policies and activities of the National Association of Counties and some of the more pressing problems in the relations between counties and the national government.

THE COUNTY AGENDA IN WASHINGTON

The National Association of Counties, formed in 1935, is the only national organization representing county government in the United States. It provides a structure through which county officials can network, exchange ideas and information, and both shape and respond to changes in public policy.[1] More broadly, it functions to educate people in Washington about the role and activities of counties in the federal system, define problems affecting counties, and help shape the federal policy agenda.

NACo began slowly as an influential participant in Washington politics. It gained some momentum in the 1950s after internal reorganization, but it did not really come into its own as a lobbying force until the 1970s, when counties became more salient nationally and were tied into federal block grant and revenue sharing programs (Haider, 1974, 32–41; Nice, 1987, 32). Since the 1970s it has often been a competitor with city organizations for scarce federal resources and service delivery responsibilities (Hale and Palley, 1981, 138).

Over the years the organization has worked for county modernization (Duncombe, 1977) and home rule.[2] At the same time it has emphasized the interdependency of American governmental units and lobbied for a greater federal role as a partner in various programs. The official goals of the organization are to improve county government, to act as a liaison between the nation's counties and other levels of government, and to serve as the national voice for county government (NACo, 1990, 1).

The diversity in county governments as to political party control, size, population density, degree of shared responsibility with other local governments, degree of autonomy, regional and geographic variations in economic base, and cultural attitudes make national representation of counties difficult. Historically, NACo has suffered from the lack of agreement among its members (Haider, 1974).

To arrive at a consensus on national policy objectives, NACo has adopted structural arrangements devised to cope with this diversity. NACo formulates policies and priorities by a process that includes the passage of resolutions by the general membership at the annual meeting, interim policy resolutions passed by the board of directors between annual meetings, and resolutions passed by steering committees to develop new policies and to carry out existing policy. Existing policies are found in the American County Platform and Resolutions approved at the annual meetings.

NACo lobbies to implement its programs. This is often done in conjunction with other public interest groups. Each group appears to have a particular base of support in Congress. By combining efforts, thus, they are sometimes able to develop a broad base of support. NACo, at one time at least, had its strongest support among suburban and Republican legislators. By combining forces with a group like the U.S. Conference of Mayors, which had strong ties to Democratic urban legislators from the Northeast and Midwest, it was able to secure broad congressional support for particular policy objectives (Hale and Palley, 1981, 57). Unity, among PIG groups, however, is not always easy to bring about. Conflicts between counties and cities over powers and revenues have been a persistent problem. As indicated earlier, such conflicts have escalated in recent years as counties have sought to adjust to a new role in the provision of urban services.

Like other public interest groups, NACo undertakes research, testifies at formal hearings, contacts individual congresspeople and administrators, and uses the media to get its message out. Often, prominent county officials present the organizations' positions. The mode of operation resembles that of private groups who attempt to influence national policy in many respects (Hale and Palley, 1981, 27–28). Success for both types of organizations is difficult to predict because it varies with such factors as the nature and timing of the demands, the availability of resources, public sentiments concerning the policies involved, lobbying skills, and the ability to enter coalitions with other groups.[3]

Generally, state and local elected officials—be they governors, mayors, or county executives—do have certain advantages over private parties in lobbying. Those who are elected on a partisan ballot have added access through their party connections. More broadly, they have an advantage in access because, to some extent, other lawmakers view them as having a legitimate right, as elected officials, to speak on behalf of their constituents (Glendening and Reeves, 1977, 50; Nice, 1987, 32). On the other hand, few people—lobbyists, lawmakers, or informed observers—view NACo and other public interest groups as having anywhere the clout enjoyed by well-financed private groups who seek access and influence through such means as campaign contributions (Achs, 1992).

Reflecting the concerns of its members, NACo naturally gives attention to programs involving the delivery of human services (Hays, 1991). Counties often administer and sometimes partially support such national programs as Aid to Families with Dependent Children, child protective services, and welfare job training. NACo keeps track of these programs. It is also concerned with changes in the Medicaid program, because in nearly 40 states county governments function as the health care provider of last resort. Welfare and Medicaid expenditures consume as much as 67 percent of some county budgets and some $14 billion annually nationwide in county taxes (NACo, 1990, 89).

Working through 12 steering committees, the association focuses on a variety of other matters of federal policy such as community and economic development, housing, homelessness, job training, transportation improvements, solid and hazardous wastes, sewage treatment, and energy (see Table 9.1).

In many respects NACo has a progressive domestic program. For example, it has urged Congress to adopt a national housing policy reaffirming a strong federal role in stimulating and underwriting affordable housing opportunities (NACo, 1990, 19); assist the structurally unemployed to acquire marketable job skills, employment, and economic self-sufficiency, thereby reducing the alternative costs of public assistance, unemployment insurance, and other income maintenance systems (NACo,

1990, 37); and to assure in some manner that all citizens have access to health care services (NACo, 1990, 73).

Many of NACo's policy positions are of particular interest to county governments in metropolitan areas faced with increasing service demands. The fact that over 75 percent of the counties in the United States are in nonmetropolitan areas, however, helps explain the strong emphasis NACo also gives to federal policy affecting agriculture and rural areas. It has, for example, generally sought refinements in legislation affecting farm price support levels, planting flexibility, and federal crop insurance; the removal of barriers to trade in foreign countries; and the adequate funding of rural development programs. Compared to the federal government, state governments play only a minimal role in most areas of agricultural policy. As one author has noted: "The federal government is really the only game in town when it comes to devising, implementing and paying for farmer benefit programs" (Rapp, 1989, 23). As indicated earlier (in Chapter 7) counties have benefited from several federal developmental programs. Direct aid to county governments in rural areas, however, has been on a sharp decline in recent years.

In pursuing the county agenda in Washington, D.C., NACo is concerned with administrative agencies and the courts as well as Congress. As Glendening and Reeves (1977, 37, quoting Farkas, 1971, 7) have pointed out, for the intergovernmental lobby: "administration has become as important as program adoption." When a public interest group "cannot change a program, it tries to alter the way it is carried out. If the organization cannot get Congress to adopt a policy an effort is made to 'maneuver it through the back door under the guise of interpretation of regulations.' " The current problem in Washington, as NACo lobbyist Edward Ferguson has pointed out, is "not just a funding issue." In addition, counties "need to be involved with the federal government in the development of rules and regulations" (Beury, 1988, 31). County officials, as we have noted, have similar complaints about the lack of access to administrators and unilateral administrative action at the state level (see Chapter 8).

Federal courts condition the problems and policies of county governments on a continuous basis. Among the major decisions in recent years have been those in *Garcia v. San Antonio* in 1985 and *South Carolina v. Baker* in 1987. In the first of these the court concluded that the question of whether the federal Fair Labor Standards Act applied to state and local employees was to be answered by Congress rather than the courts. As the result of such rulings, Congress has been free to impose costly mandates on state and local governments. In the South Carolina case, the high court

Table 9.1
NACo Steering Committees and National Policy Jurisdictions

STEERING COMMITTEE	NATIONAL POLICY JURISDICTION	
Agriculture and Rural Affairs	a. Farm legislation affecting the economy of agricultural counties b. Farm credit policies c. Trade legislation affecting agriculture	d. Rural development programs e. Soil conservation f. Agricultural land preservation
Community and Economic Development	a. General community development and redevelopment b. Residential, commercial, and industrial development c. Housing programs	d. Building and housing codes e. Subdivision regulation f. Public works and economic development
Employment	a. Employment and training programs b. Youth and public service employment c. Vocational education d. Migrant and native American programs	e. Rural manpower f. Employment security g. Unemployment insurance
Environment, Energy, and Land Use	a. Air, water, and noise pollution control b. Solid and hazardous waste management and disposal c. Energy use	d. Land use - comprehensive planning, coastal zone management, growth management, energy facilities siting and creation
Health	a. Health care delivery and financing (including Medicare and Medicaid) affecting local health	b. Mental health (including drug and alcohol abuse) programs, services, facilities, and financing
Human Services and Education	a. Welfare reform, income maintenance b. Food stamps, low-income energy assistance c. Rights of handicapped d. Deinstitutionalization	e. Illegal aliens and refugees f. Domestic violence g. Administration of county welfare Programs h. Health care delivery
Intergovernmental Relations	a. Home rule and regionalism - county structures, procedures, and management b. Intergovernmental relations between counties and subdivisions, state and national governments	c. Liability and insurance

Justice and Public Safety
a. Criminal justice planning
b. Law enforcement, courts, corrections
c. Firearm control
d. Organized crime
e. Juvenile justice and delinquency
f. Emergency management
g. Fire prevention and control
h. Civil disturbances

Labor and Employee Benefits
a. Personnel and policy practices
b. Merit systems
c. Equal employment opportunity
d. Collective bargaining and unionization
e. Wages, salaries, pensions, fringe benefits
f. Occupational safety and health
g. Workers' compensation
h. Social security
i. Intergovernmental personnel act programs

Public Lands
a. All matters related to federally owned lands
b. Tax immunity problems
c. Federal land management programs

Taxation and Finance
a. All matters of financial resources of counties
b. Federal assistance
c. Municipal borrowing
d. County revenues
e. Federal budget
f. Federal grants
g. Tax reform

Transportation
a. Comprehensive transportation planning
b. Highway finance and safety
c. Public transit development and finance
d. Airport development, noise, and safety
e. Railways and waterways
f. Special problems of handicapped and elderly

Source: Adapted from National Association of Counties (1990).

also told state and local governments that their only protection against restrictions on their use of tax-exempt financing is through the congressional political process. NACo and other public interest groups have been very concerned over U.S. Supreme Court decisions that have eroded state and local protections against the expansion of congressional authority. They contend that the Tenth Amendment to the U.S. Constitution is a major substantive limit on national power and should be so viewed by the courts.

PARTNERSHIPS, MONEY, AND MANDATES

Many of the planks in NACo's county platform call for an improved intergovernmental approach or partnership to various problems. The association argues, for example, that the federal, state, and local governments share responsibility in providing a sound, balanced, and coordinated national transportation system. This system includes highways, public transit, airports, waterways, and railroads. The association views the lack of federal funding for these systems in recent years as having had a significant negative impact on the economic well-being of the entire nation. On environmental matters, NACo views "counties and cities as the primary service deliverer, states as coordinators, and the federal government as responsible for setting minimum standards, conducting research, and providing financial and technical assistance" (NACo, 1990, 49). The recommended intergovernmental approach to law enforcement follows similar lines:

> It is only through a county partnership with the other levels of government in the American system of federalism that a full-scale comprehensive approach may be taken to crime and public safety problems. Counties must increasingly look to the federal government for substantial amounts of financial assistance; to the states for coordination of state crime and public safety programs with those of local areas, and for appropriate statutory authorizations and a measure of financial assistance; and to their sister municipal governments and regional agencies for cooperative and coordinated local approaches to these problems (NACo, 1990, 137).

The central problem from the county point of view is that the federal government has largely abandoned its role as an intergovernmental partner. In the Reagan White House, cutbacks in domestic programs were seen as a matter of "defunding the left" and of reducing subsides for selfish special interests groups (Reed, 1983; Levine and Thurber, 1986).

County governments have been particularly hard hit by declines in federal aid in recent years (see Figure 9.1). From 1985 to 1988 federal aid to all local governments declined from $21.7 billion to $17.1 billion, or about 21 percent. The loss for counties in this period was from $4.7 billion to $2.6 billion or nearly 44 percent ("Intergovernmental Digest," 1990, 23–24). Several social programs have been cut. The loss of the General Revenue Sharing program started in 1972 and phased out in 1987 created revenue problems in every county.

Along with spending cuts, counties have been adversely affected by changes in federal tax policies and regulatory polices. Congress in recent years has taken several steps to improve its revenues without increasing taxes. In taking such steps, however, it has sometimes ignored the direct and indirect linkages between federal and local tax systems. Changes in federal taxation policy such as eliminating the deductability of sales taxes from the U.S. income tax, for example, have negative effects on the ability of state and local governments to raise revenues. So too have recent national increases in the gasoline, tobacco, beer, wine, and distilled spirits taxes.

To further complicate matters, the national government has forced state and local governments, including counties, to absorb the costs of complying with expensive federal government mandates. The change in federal policy from using subsidies to regulatory mandates to encourage states and localities to take various courses of action began in the mid-1970s. One repercussion of this change in policy has been increased costs. In 1988, federal mandates were estimated to have cost state and local governments some $100 billion a year (Calmes, 1988). More recently, the Florida League of Cities has estimated that state and local governments spend up to 24 percent of their budgets on federal mandates (Mack, 1992, S3490). Expensive federal mandates occur in policy areas such as air and water quality, solid waste, hazardous waste, transportation standards, courts and corrections, and health services (R. Thomas, 1991, 11). County officials have reacted with the cry: "Congress, don't pass the buck without the buck!" (D. M. Stewart, 1991, 19).

CONCLUSION

The image of state and local officials as being simply another set of special pleaders with particularly large appetites, rather than uniquely constituted cogovernors or partners, began to take root in Washington during the early 1970s with the growth of the intergovernmental lobby (Haider, 1974; Levine and Thurber, 1986; Stanfield, 1976). For political

Figure 9.1
Federal Intergovernmental Revenues, by Type of Local Government, Fiscal Years 1979–88

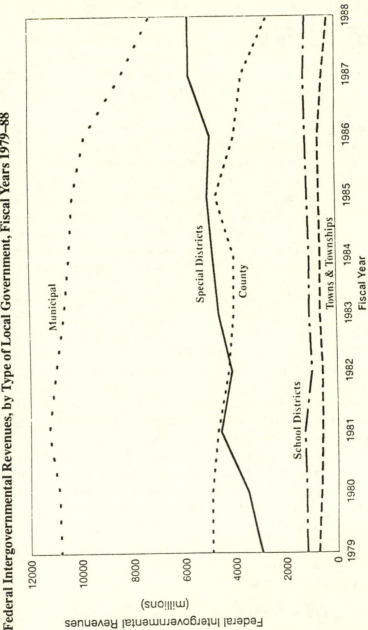

Source: Intergovernmental Perspective/Fall 1990, p. 24.

scientists, PIGs became viewed like other groups—as operating in a closed cozy subsystem or as part of a "iron triangle" in which they and particular congressional committees and administrative agencies worked out policies of mutual benefit (Hale and Palley, 1981; Levine and Thurber, 1986; Reed, 1983). By the late 1970s these negative views and increasing fiscal problems at the national level led to cuts in grant programs. With Reagan, the process of destabilizing the PIGs and subgovernments of which they were a part accelerated. Faced with a hostile administration, the "iron triangle" began to collapse.

In recent years the costs of government have been shifted to state and local governments. This has happened both directly though mandates from the federal government requiring state and local governments to pick up certain costs, and indirectly, through the ability of local constituencies to force state and local governments to at least partially make up for the funds lost by federal spending cuts out of their own revenues.

County governments and the organizations that represent them have not given up entirely on the renewal of the federal-local partnership. NACo and other public interest groups, for example, have called for a national Local Partnership Act, which would reorder national priorities, giving state and local governments a share of the "peace dividend" brought about by a relaxation in international tensions. As one leading county official, D. Michael Stewart (1991, 19), has put it: "If county officials could have their dreams come true," they "would begin with a federal attitude that would view local government as a partner in an intergovernmental system, not as a special interest." Stewart also warns: "The federal system cannot function effectively if local government must wait in line for the favor and attention of the Congress and the President. Local officials are elected to do the business of government. Local government is not a private interest or a corporation" (19).

NOTES

1. An example of how networking groups like NACo make it possible for local officials to respond to sudden and unexpected changes in judicial policy is found in Johnston and Kurtz (1986).

2. In regard to home rule, NACo argues:

1. State constitutions and statutes should provide for flexibility of form, function, and finance. In this manner, the authority of the county government will be based on *implied* powers and thus allow it to finance all areas except those expressly prohibited.

2. Counties should be free to devise their own internal organizational structure, either under charter or under general law.

3. Counties should be free to determine the scope and extent of the governmental service each will render, subject to the recognized need for some uniformity in the standard of delivery of services of national or statewide impact.

4. Counties should be free to devise their own operating policies in all governmental programs, including those financed wholly or substantially by federal or state funds, subject to a requirement that such policies be definitely set forth in writing.

5. Counties should have the ability to employ means of financing county government with stable and diversified revenue sources that are not prohibited by preemption (NACo, 1990, 119).

3. Glendening and Reeves (1977, 36) note:

Both public and private interest groups employ a wide variety of strategies, too numerous to mention here, depending on the program or policy they are trying to influence. Their activities are prescribed by the prevailing public sentiment about the program or policy and the timing of their demands, the acceptance of the particular groups as a legitimate voice for the interests purportedly represented, their reputations and those of their lobbyists, and the resources they can command in terms of membership finances, and contacts are also determinative of success. Important, too, are the coalitions they can develop with other organizations concerned with the same subject, as well as the opposition they encounter.

Chapter 10

Counties, Other Governments, and the Future

David R. Berman

Governments in the United States share powers and functions. One consequence of this sharing is that they regularly bump into each other. "With each bump," Thomas Anton (1989, 2) notes, "an opportunity is provided to challenge or affirm existing understandings regarding who should do what, on whose budget."

The future of county governments in the United States, accordingly, is likely to be one of instability caused by the constant interaction with other governments and the recurring adjustment of responsibilities. Interaction takes place on two planes: a horizontal one in which counties interact with municipalities and other units of local government, and a vertical one in which counties are in contact with state governments and the federal government, both of which have the advantage of operating from higher levels of legal authority.

This concluding chapter looks at the two sets of relationships and what the future may bring in regard to the roles, responsibilities, and performance of county governments.

COUNTIES AND THE SYSTEM OF LOCAL GOVERNMENT

"To put the matter bluntly, government in the United States is chaotic" (Grodzins, 1964). These were the thoughts of political scientist Morton Grodzins nearly 30 years ago. Grodzins referred to both the large number of governments in the United States and the complicated set of relationships among them. Most of the governments are local units. All together there are better than 83,000 of them.

Using theory based on the behavior of nation-states in the international system, each local government in a metropolitan area or region follows its own definition of what is in its self-interest. Each government looks to maintain its legal autonomy and territorial integrity and to compete effectively with other units for scarce resources such as profitable business enterprises and high-income residents. Competition may produce conflict, bordering on war, but enlightened self-interest also brings diplomatic relations, treaties, agreements, and other cooperative endeavors to avoid conflict or solve common problems (Holden, 1964; V. Jones, 1957; Kincaid, 1989).

How do counties relate to this pattern of activity? As indicated in the previous chapters, they perform a variety of services—sometimes looking like cities and sometimes looking simply like the administrators of state programs. On one hand, they contribute to the confusion, competition, and overlap one finds in the pattern of local government. On the other hand, and far more importantly, counties often function as key elements in the cooperative system or the network of local governments that holds the system together and, in many parts of country, are major providers of areawide services.

Counties participate in various types of cooperative undertakings. They supply services under contract to municipal governments and jointly plan, finance, or deliver services on the basis of agreements with other local governments.[1] Counties also participate with other local units in various metropolitan or regional associations. Counties around the country have assumed responsibilities from municipal governments in such areas as jails, libraries, and street repairs in order to end duplication of services and effect economies of scale. Also increasingly shifted to counties are regionally important services such as transit, solid waste, and health. Indeed, as one authority has noted: "If counties had not existed at the beginning of the decade, something like them would probably have been invented by the end of it to deliver sub-regional and regional services" (Dodge, 1990, 358).

Reformers who wish to shift governmental responsibilities to multipurpose, politically accountable entities with broad, metropolitan or regional jurisdictions, naturally think first of county governments. Compared to municipalities, the larger jurisdictions of counties make them potentially better able to deal with problems such as environmental protection and transportation. Compared to special authorities, counties are well-known general-purpose governments directly accountable to the voters. Shifting responsibilities to the county often provides a broader focus, economies of scale, and a more stable and equitable tax base. Counties, too, are in a particularly good position to provide redistributive programs (see Chapter 6).

One approach to making greater use of the county is simply to transfer functions to it on a piecemeal basis, as has been done in various parts of the country over the last several decades. Alternatively, reformers could increase county responsibility substantially through charter reorganization. Using the Dade County, Florida, model, reformers could create a two-tier or federated system in which counties perform various activities considered best provided on an areawide basis, while municipal governments assume more specialized local functions.

A federated system would probably be easier to bring about than a complete one-tier consolidation of city and county governments because less change is involved. State legislatures may require the consolidation of two or more local units simply by legislation and without the requirement of a popular vote in the jurisdictions involved. The 1970 merger of Indianapolis and Marion County, Indiana, occurred in this manner. More often, however, proposals to consolidate city and county governments require public approval in the jurisdictions affected. Proposals are likely to fail at the polls. In recent years, four out of every five proposals have been voted down (Ward, 1992, 30).[2] With these failures, reformers have turned away from consolidation as a remedy to metropolitan problems and toward more cooperative approaches.

The need to improve regional problem solving is likely to be a dominant theme of the 1990s. Counties are likely to feel the pressure to improve their role as partners and to assume even more areawide functions. In many sprawling areas, however, counties may already be obsolete as natural regional entities. In these situations a multipurpose governing entity whose jurisdiction covers two or more counties is called for. Councils of Government (COGs) may serve as the building blocks for this type of entity. Portland, Oregon's, Metropolitan Service District, a multipurpose government run by officials directly elected by the voters, serves as a prototype. The full development of councils as viable units of regional government, however, awaits large-scale efforts to increase citizen participation in the governing system (Henderson, 1990). An alternative to improving COGs is the creation of a new level of local government, sitting above the counties, such as that recently proposed by reformers in California ("Counties Are Out of Date," 1991).

In the real world, counties and other local governments are not totally like autonomous nation-states. As part of the vertical system they are subject to control from above. Regionalism may be imposed from the top down rather than result from the bottom up effort of local units. Indeed, in many states regional cooperation is mandated by state law. A growing number of states, for example, require counties and other local governments to work together in preparing multipurpose regional plans relating to growth management, environmental protection, and an adequate infrastructure that meet minimum state standards (Shanahan, 1991). Unfortunately, such requirements have, at times, ignored limitations on the ability of counties and municipal governments to do the job (Decker, 1987).

COUNTY, STATE, AND NATION

Counties, as participants in the system of vertical federalism, find their financial status, authority, and obligations greatly conditioned by the federal government and, even more so, by state governments.

Counties and other local governments have long benefited from the system of federal aid. One of the more distressing facts of life to many local officials, however, is that federal aid has declined since the late 1970s. As we have noted, the growth of costly mandates has made matters doubly difficult for county officials. County governments, being at the end of the path of "one way federalism," wind up paying many of these mandated costs. Thus, when Congress decides to increase Medicaid coverage, it forces the states to pay more for their share of the increased costs (or risk losing the program), but state governments do so by passing the increased costs on to counties or other local governments (Todd, 1991).

State governments have always been the prime intergovernmental actor in the life of county governments. Since the late 1970s they have become even more important to the everyday functioning of counties. Counties have turned to their states for help in making up for revenues lost because of declines in federal aid. State aid over the past several years has been spotty—varying from state to state—and unreliable. During the late 1980s and early 1990s, times of economic stress in most states, not only did aid diminish, but the states increasingly responded to their own difficulties by mandating that counties and municipalities pick up the bill for expensive programs.

Over the past several decades, more states have authorized county home rule, and legislatures have given counties more discretion—for example, in regard to how they wish to structure their governments. State governments have even allowed county governments more discretion in regard to revenue sources. Yet, because of mandates and increased demands, counties have had to increase property taxes. The property tax, in turn, has become the nation's least popular tax (U.S. Advisory Commission, 1991). With increases in this tax has come the threat of a new taxpayer rebellion.

State legislators, regardless of the nature of their constituencies, ideologies, or party identification, have been reluctant to relinquish a great deal of their control over counties. Attitudes concerning state-county relations seem to be very much a product of Miles' Law: "Where you stand depends on where you sit" (Miles, 1978). From where they sit, county officials usually see more county autonomy to be a good thing. From where they sit, state legislators often see more county autonomy as something that might bring undesirable results (Berman, Martin, and Kajfez, 1985). Various businesses and other groups also worry about the effects of giving local governments more discretion. They find it easier and more comfortable to deal with a single state legislative body than with a multitude of local governmental authorities.

Because of the inferior legal status of local governments, states have virtually unlimited ability to intervene in county affairs by stipulating rules and requirements and by mandating that certain functions be performed. Intervention has been a norm because state officials are apt to view counties in their traditional role as administrative units for the execution of state policy. Yet, as Tanis Salant has noted (in Chapter 8), there are some signs that such attitudes may be breaking down.

The recurring problem for county officials in the vertical system is finding means of influencing federal and state policies so as to maximize local authority and the ability of local governments to meet citizen demands for services. County officials have had some success over the years, working both directly and through various organizations such as National Association of County Officials and county associations (see Chapters 8 and 9; Cigler, 1991a).

Public interest organizations like NACo and county associations and those representing cities and towns, it should be noted, most directly represent the interests of particular existing units of local government. These interests may or may not be the same as the interests of the larger metropolitan or regional area (Farkas, 1971). It may also be the case that what local officials want done is quite different from what federal or state legislators who live in the same jurisdictions feel is desirable public policy or in the interests of their constituents (Calmes, 1988).

Securing policy objectives at the federal and state level has been particularly difficult for public interest groups in recent years. This has been due in part to a general economic downturn. Convincing federal and state lawmakers to assume responsibility for problems, rather than dismiss them as being local in nature, is a difficult task even in the best of times.

As economic stress increases, local officials can expect not only declining intergovernmental aid but increased costly mandates. As an ACIR (1990, 2) study has noted: "In the absence of sufficient funds—whether by legislative choice or economic constraint—there is a strong temptation to satisfy policy demands by mandating that functions be performed by other governments."

County and other local officials do not look upon themselves as special pleaders, but as spokespersons "for semi-sovereign subnational governments rendering the bulk of the nation's domestic services and functions" (Walker, 1986). They prefer the status of governmental partner rather than just another "special interest." Gaining or regaining this status depends in large part on the existence of a strong economy, nationally and in various states. It also requires a change in more fundamental attitudes in Washington and state capitols, regarding the status and roles of local government.

THE FUTURE: ARE COUNTIES READY?

"Counties can be viewed as the last frontier in local government and a new frontier for professional public administration," wrote Claude D. Malone, County Administrator, Montgomery County, Ohio, in 1986. The last frontier of local government is on the metropolitan or regional level. Counties in many parts of the country have assumed a leading role performing functions that are metropolitan or regional in nature. This role is likely to grow. On this last frontier, however, counties share the stage with a variety of interjurisdictional bodies, some of which, such as Councils of Government, may gain considerable importance as the decade unfolds.

Other than directly providing areawide services, counties are destined to become even more active as partners in interlocal networks, vital units within a larger system of regional governance, and as administrative units for state designed programs.

Improving the performance of counties in all of their roles depends, in part, on making them more streamlined, professional, capable, resource-rich, and creditable entities. As noted in previous chapters, much progress has already been made toward these goals, especially in metropolitan areas, with structural changes designed to centralize authority and through the hiring of professionally trained personnel. County governments in nonmetropolitan areas have also improved professionally and are likely to continue to do so. For many counties, but especially those serving rural communities, an important alternative to building administrative capacity is expansion of the system of interlocal cooperation—that is, sharing and doing more things with other local governments (Seroka, 1988).

The increased professionalism of administration has made it easier for counties to cooperate with neighboring jurisdictions because they are often run by people with essentially the same training and outlooks. Indeed, Vincent L. Marando and Mavis Mann Reeves (1991, 224) have concluded: "Differentials between the professional competences of counties and cities need no longer stand in the way of effective partnerships. Professional parity between county and city administrators fosters communication, increased interaction, and the search for joint approaches to problem solving."

Some counties, however, continue to suffer from what one authority calls the "tism's and the ism's—nepotism, favoritism, junketism, pork barrelism, perkism, patronism" (Malone, 1986, 5). Despite improvements, moreover, the image of counties as do-nothing governments has been a difficult one to shake. To doubters there is a feeling, as noted by the U.S. ACIR (1972, 42) some time ago, "that even if county governments were given the power and authority to become more responsive to previous problems, the initiative would be lacking—that the parochial interest of county governments precludes any effective response."

County officials reject these views, contending that they are willing and able, both politically and administratively, to undertake new responsibilities. They do, however, agree that the lack of state financial support severely limits their ability to perform. Many county officials would like to see a restoration of federal funds (Streib and Waugh, 1991a; Waugh and Streib, 1990; Waugh, 1988; and Waugh and Hy, 1988). Yet few county officials expect drastic changes in federal aid policies in the immediate future. With less federal financial support and increased demands for services, county officials must work to strengthen the state-local partnership.

Are counties prepared for the future? As several contributors to this volume suggest, capacity in the counties has been slow to develop. Though things may be changing, county officials seem largely reluctant to exercise the authority they now have or to challenge state authority. Ultimately the capacity and the performance of counties depend not only on what authority and resources other governments make available, but on the willingness of county officials to help themselves.

NOTES

1. NACo's surveys show a huge growth in intergovernmental agreements in recent years (Ward, 1992, 32–33). Counties and municipalities in metropolitan

areas have been particularly active in regard to contracts. Recent increase in this activity has been driven chiefly by cost considerations (Morgan and Hirlinger, 1991).

2. There have been only 28 city-county consolidations in over 200 years, though ten of these have taken place in the last 20 years (Ward, 1992, 30).

References

Achs, Nicole. 1992. "Clout." *American City and County* (May): 79–81.

Aderlfer, Harold F. 1975. *Pennsylvania Local Government 1681–1974*. State College, PA: Penns Valley Publishers.

Adrian, Charles R. 1967. *State and Local Governments*. New York: McGraw-Hill Book Company.

Anton, Thomas J. 1989. *American Federalism and Public Policy: How the System Works*. New York: Random House.

Barrows, R., and L. Libby, eds. 1981. *Local Agricultural Land Policies: Cases from the Midwest*. Ames: North Central Regional Center for Rural Development, Iowa State University.

Bayless, Betsey. 1992. "1992 Chairman's Address." Maricopa County Board of Supervisors (January 6).

Beer, Samuel H. 1977. "Political Overload and Federalism." *Polity* 10 (Fall): 5–17.

Bender, Lewis and Thaddeus C. Zolty. 1986. "Rapid Growth: Impacts on the Politics and Administration of Rural Governments." In Jim Seroka, ed., *Rural Public Administration: Problems and Prospects*. Westport, Conn.: Greenwood Press.

Bender, Lloyd D., B. L. Green, T. F. Hady, J. A. Kuehn, M. K. Nelson, L. B. Perkinson, and P. J. Ross. 1985. *The Diverse Social and Economic Structure of Nonmetropolitan America*. Washington, D.C.: U.S. Department of Agriculture, Economic Research Service, Rural Development Research Report Number 49 (September).

Benton, J. Edwin and Donald C. Menzel. 1990. "The Changing Service Scope of County Governments: The Case of Florida." Paper delivered at the Annual Meeting of the American Political Science Association, San Francisco, August 28–September 2.

_____. 1991a. "County Service Trends and Practices: The Case of Florida." *State and Local Government Review* (forthcoming).

_____. 1991b. "Contracting and Franchising County Services in Florida." *Urban Affairs Quarterly* (forthcoming).

Benton, J. Edwin and Platon N. Rigos. 1985. "Patterns of Metropolitan Service Dominance: Central City and Central County Service Roles Compared." *Urban Affairs Quarterly* 20 (March): 285–302.

Berman, David R. 1989. "State Actions Affecting Local Governments: Involvement, Problems, and Relationships." *The Municipal Yearbook 1989.* Washington, D.C.: International City Management Association.

Berman, David R. and Lawrence L. Martin. 1988. "State-Local Relations: An Examination of Local Discretion." *Public Administration Review* 48 (March/April): 637–641.

Berman, David R., Lawrence L. Martin, and Laura Kajfez. 1985. "County Home Rule: Does Where You Stand Depend on Where You Sit?" *State and Local Government Review* (Spring 1985): 232–234.

Beury, Kim. 1988. "Counties Hopeful for New Deal." *American City and County* (August): 30–34.

Bollens, John C. et al. 1969. *American County Government.* Beverly Hills, Calif.: Sage Publications.

Bollens, John C. 1978. *Special District Government in the United States.* Westport, Conn.: Greenwood Press.

Braaten, Kaye. 1991. "Rural Counties: The Challenges Ahead." *Intergovernmental Perspective* 17 (Winter): 38–40.

Bragg, John T. 1988. "A View from the Commission." *Intergovernmental Perspective* (Summer): 2.

Brown, Anthony. 1980. "Technical Assistance to Rural Communities: Stopgap or Capacity Building?" *Public Administration Review* 40 (January/February): 18–23.

Brown, David L. and Kenneth L. Deavers. 1987. "Rural Changes and the Rural Economic Development Policy Agenda for the 1980s." In *Rural Economic Development in the 1980s.* Washington, D.C.: U.S. Department of Agriculture, Economic Research Service, ERS Staff Report AGES870724. (July): 1–8.

Burgess, Philip M. 1975. "Capacity Building and the Elements of Public Management." *Public Administration Review* (Special Issue, December).

Calmes, Jacqueline. 1988. "444 North Capitol Street: Where State Lobbyists Are Learning Coalition Politics." *Governing* (February): 17–21.

Chicoine, David L. and Norman Walzer. 1985. *Government Structure and Local Public Finance.* Boston: Oelgeschlager, Gunn, and Hain.

Cigler, Beverly A. 1979. "Local Growth Management: Changing Assumptions About Land." *The Urban Interest* (Fall): 52–58.

_____. 1984."Small City and Rural Governance: The Changing Environment." *Public Administration Review* 44 (November/December): 540–545.

_____. 1986. "Small Cities' Policy Responses to the New Federalism." In Lewis G. Bender and James A. Stever, eds., *Administering the New Federalism*. Boulder, Colo.: Westview Press.

_____. 1989. "Trends Affecting Local Administrators." In James L. Perry, ed., *Handbook of Public Administration*. San Francisco: Jossey-Bass.

_____. 1990. "County Contracting: Reconciling the Accountability and Information Paradoxes." *Public Administration Quarterly* 14 (Fall): 285–301.

_____.1991a. "The County-State Connection: A National Study of Associations of Counties." Paper presented to the Annual Meeting of the American Political Science Association, Washington, D.C.

_____. 1991b. *Meeting Fiscal Challenges in the 1990s: Innovative Approaches for Rural Local Governments*. Harrisburg: Center for Rural Pennsylvania (June).

Cotter, Cornelius P., James L. Gibson, John F. Bibby, and Robert J. Huckshorn. 1984. *Party Organization in American Politics*. New York: Praeger.

"Counties Are Out of Date in California." 1991. *State Legislatures*, March: 9.

Crane, W. and A. C. Hagensick. 1976. *Wisconsin Government and Politics*. Madison: Institute of Governmental Affairs, The University of Wisconsin.

Davis, B. 1991. "Coping in the Ungovernable County." Paper presented to the Conference on Facilitative Leadership, April 12–13, Public Administrative Program, North Carolina State University, Raleigh.

Decker, Jane Elizabeth. 1987. "Management and Organizational Capacities for Responding to Growth in Florida's Nonmetropolitan Counties." *Journal of Urban Affairs* 9: 47–61.

DeGrove, John and Carol Lawrence. 1977. "County Government Service Delivery." In Linda Ganschinietz, ed., *Decade of Decisions: 1976–1986*. Washington, D.C.: National Association of Counties.

DeSantis, Victor S. 1989. "County Government: A Century of Change." In *The Municipal Year Book 1989*. Washington, D.C.: International City Management Association, 55–84.

DeSantis, Victor S. and Tari Renner. 1992a. "The Impact of Political Structures upon Public Policies in American Counties." Paper presented at the 1992 Midwest Political Science Association Meeting, Chicago, April 9–11.

_____.1992b. "Minority and Gender Representation in American County Legislatures: The Effect of Election Systems." In Joseph Zimmerman and Wilma Rule, eds., *The Impact of U.S. Electoral Systems on Minorities and Women*. Westport, Conn.: Greenwood Press.

_____. 1989. "Minority and Sexual Representation in American County Legislatures: The Effect of Election System." Paper presented at the annual meeting of the American Political Science Association, Atlanta, August 31–September 3.

Dodge, William R. 1990. "Regional Problem Solving in the 1990s: Experimen-
   tation with Local Governance for the 21st Century." *National Civic
   Review* (July/August): 354–366.

Downs, Anthony. 1973. *Opening Up the Suburbs: An Urban Strategy for America.* New Haven, Conn.: Yale University Press.

_____. 1985. "The Future of Industrial Cities." In Paul E. Peterson, ed., *The
   New Urban Reality.* Washington, D.C.: The Brookings Institution.

Duncombe, Herbert S. 1977. *Modern County Government.* Washington, D.C.:
   National Association of Counties.

Ebel, Robert D. 1991. "A Profile of County Finances." *Intergovernmental
   Perspective* (Winter): 14–17.

Effross, Harris I. 1975. *County Governing Bodies in New Jersey: Reorganization and Reform of Boards of Chosen Freeholders, 1798–1974.* New
   Brunswick, N.J.: Rutgers University Press.

Ehrenhalt, Alan. 1991. *The United States of Ambition: Politicians, Power, and
   the Pursuit of Office.* New York: Random House.

Facwett, James A. 1986. "Redefining Local Government Power: The Influence
   of Informal Powers in Challenging Joint Implementation of a State
   Coastal Plan." *Policy Studies Review* 6: 330–339.

Fairlie, John A. 1906. *Local Government in Counties, Towns and Villages.* New
   York: The Century Company.

Fairlie, John A. and Charles M. Kneier. 1930. *County Government and Administration.* New York: D. Appleton-Century Co.

Farkas, Suzane. 1971. *Urban Lobbying: Mayors in the Federal Arena.* New
   York: New York University Press.

Fehr, Stephen C. and D'Vera Cohn. 1990. "Census Shows Montgomery
   Maryland's Biggest Jurisdiction." *Washington Post* (August 26): A1,
   A4.

Fishman, Robert. 1987. *Bourgeois Utopias: The Rise and Fall of Suburbia.* New
   York: Basic Books.

_____. 1990. "America's New City: Megalopolis Unbound." *Wilson Quar-
   terly* (Winter): 24–45.

Flora, Jan L., J. J. Chriss, E. Gale, G. P. Green, F. E. Schmidt, and C. Flora.
   1991. *From the Grassroots: Profiles of 103 Rural Self-Development
   Projects.* Washington, D.C.: Economic Research, USDA Agriculture
   and Rural Economy Division, AGES 9123 (April).

Fosler, R. Scott. 1991. "The Suburban County: Governing Mainstream Diversity." *Intergovernmental Perspective* (Winter): 33–37.

Frendreis, John P., James L. Gibson, and Laura L. Vertz. 1990. "The Electoral
   Relevance of Local Party Organizations." *American Political Science
   Review* 48 (March): 225–235.

Frisbie, W. Parker and John D. Kasarda. 1988. "Spatial Processes." In Neil
   Smelser, ed., *Handbook of Sociology.* Newbury Park, CA: Sage Publications.

Gargan, John J. 1981. "Consideration of Local Government Capacity." *Public Administration Review* 41 (November/December): 649–658.

Garnick, Daniel H. 1988. "Local Area Economic Growth Patterns: A Comparison of the 1980s and Previous Decades." In Michael G. McGeary and Laurence E. Lynn, Jr., eds., *Urban Change and Poverty*. Washington, D.C.: National Academy Press.

Gilbert, Charles E. 1967. *Governing the Suburbs*. Bloomington: Indiana University Press.

Gilbertson, H. L. 1917. *The County: The "Dark Continent" of American Politics*. New York: The National Short Ballot Organization.

Giles, William A., Gerald T. Gabris, and Dale A. Krane. 1980. "Dynamics in Rural Policy Development: The Uniqueness of County Government." *Public Administration Review* 40 (January):24–28.

Giventer, L. L. and W. E. Neeley. 1984. "County Problem and Decision-Making Perceptions: California Supervisors Compared with Georgia and Florida Commissioners."*Public Administration Quarterly* 7: 498–516.

Glendening, Parris N. and Mavis Mann Reeves. 1977. *Pragmatic Federalism*. Pacific Palisades, Calif.: Palisades Publishers.

Goche, James. 1987. "Has It Ever Been Easy?" *American City & County* 102: 64–71.

Gold, Steven D. 1988. "The State of State-Local Relations." *State Legislatures* (August): 17–20.

Grodzins, Morton. 1964. "Centralization and Decentralization in the American Federal System." In Robert A. Goldwin, ed., *A Nation of States*. Chicago: Public Affairs Conference Center.

Gurwitt, Rob. 1989. "Cultures Clash as Old-Time Politics Confronts Button-Down Management." *Governing* 2(7): 42–48.

_____. 1991. "The Empowering of the Suburbs." *Governing* 4(5): 58–63.

Haider, Donald H. 1974. *When Governments Come to Washington*. New York: The Free Press.

Hale, George E. and Marian Lief Palley. 1991. *The Politics of Federal Grants*. Washington, D.C.: Congressional Quarterly Press.

Hall, John S. and Richard A. Eribes. 1985. "The Reagan Domestic Program from the Arizona Perspective." Tempe: Arizona State University.

Hamilton, Christopher and Donald T. Wells. 1990. *Federalism, Power, and Political Economy*. Englewood Cliffs, NJ: Prentice-Hall.

Hanson, B. L. 1965. "County Commissioners of Oklahoma." *Midwest Journal of Political Science* 9: 388–400.

Hawkins, Robert B. 1990. "ACIR Roundtable on International Economic Competitiveness." *Intergovernmental Perspective* 16 (Winter): 5–17, 23–24.

Hays, R. Allen. 1991. "Intergovernmental Lobbying: Toward an Understanding of Issue Priorities." *The Western Political Quarterly* 44 (December): 1081–1098.

Henderson, Lenneal J. 1990. "Metropolitan Governance: Citizen Participation in the Urban Federation." *National Civil Review* 79 (March/April): 105–117.

Herbers, John. 1990. "The Growing Role of the States Is Greater Than We Knew." *Governing* (March): 11.

Hines, R. L., and T. L. Napier. 1985. "Factors Affecting Local Public Officials' Decisions to Seek Reelection." *Journal of the Community Development Society* 16: 54–79.

Hirsch, Paul M. 1987. "Evolution of the Atlanta MSA." *Urban Resources* (Winter): A1–A4.

Holden, Matthew. 1964. "The Governance of the Metropolis as a Problem in Diplomacy." *Journal of Politics* 26: 627–647.

Honadle, Beth W. 1981. "A Capacity-Building Framework: A Search for Concept and Purpose." *Public Administration Review* 41 (September/October): 575–580.

_____. 1984. *Capacity-Building Management Improvement for Local Governments: An Annotated Bibliography,* RDRR-28, Washington, D.C.: U. S. Department of Agriculture, Economic Statistics Services (March).

"Intergovernmental Digest." 1990. In *Intergovernmental Perspective* Fall: 23–24.

Jeffery, Blake R., Tanis J. Salant, and Alan L. Boroshok. 1989. *County Government Structure: A State by State Report.* Washington, D.C.: National Association of Counties.

John, Dewitt, Sandra S. Batie, and Kim Norris. 1988. *A Brighter Future for Rural America? Strategies for Communities and States.* Washington, D.C.: National Governor's Association.

Johnston, Van R. and Maxine Kurtz. 1986. "Handling a Public Policy Emergency: The Fair Labor Standards Act in the Public Sector." *Public Administration Review* (September/ October): 414–422.

Jones, Victor. 1957. "The Organization of a Metropolitan Region." *University of Pennsylvania Law Review* 105: 539.

Jones, William A., Jr. and C. Bradley Doss. 1978. "Local Officials' Reaction to Federal 'Capacity-Building.' " *Public Administration Review* (January/February): 64–69.

Kajfez, Laura J., John S. Hall, and Albert K. Karnig. 1984. "Counties in the National Context." In John S. Hall and Albert K. Karnig, eds., *County Government in Arizona: Challenges of the 1980s.* Phoenix: The Arizona Academy.

Kasarda, John D. 1978. "Urbanization, Community, and the Metropolitan Problem." In David Street and Associates, eds., *Handbook of Contemporary Urban Life.* San Francisco: Jossey-Bass.

_____. 1985. "Urban Change and Minority Opportunities." In Paul E. Peterson, ed., *The New Urban Reality.* Washington, D.C.: The Brookings Institution.

Kincaid, John. 1989. "Metropolitan Governance: Reviving International and Market Analogies." *Intergovernmental Perspective* (Spring): 23–27.

Klinger, Ann. 1991. "County Leadership and Models for Change." *Intergovernmental Perspective* 17 (Winter): 45–48.

Koehler, C. T. 1983. *Managing California Counties*. Sacramento: County Supervisors Association of California.

Kraemer, Richard L. and Charldean Newell. 1990. *Texas Politics*. 4th ed. St. Paul: West.

Lease, M. H., Jr. 1977. "County Government: Structure, Problems, and Reform." In M. L. Gieske and E. R. Brandt, eds., *Perspectives on Minnesota Government and Politics*. Iowa: Kendall/Hunt Publishing, 341–350.

Levine, Charles H. and James A. Thurber. 1986. "Reagan and the Intergovernmental Lobby: Iron Triangles, Cozy Subsystems and Political Conflict." In Allan J. Cigler and Burdett A. Loomis, eds., *Interest Group Politics*, 2nd ed. Washington, D.C.: Congressional Quarterly Press, 202–220.

Lewis, Edward B. 1986. "Urban Versus Rural Management: The Case of County Administrator Counties in the United States." In Jim Seroka, ed., *Rural Public Administration: Problems and Prospects*. Westport, Conn.: Greenwood Press, 77–94.

Lima, J. T., and J. Woolley. 1990. "Local Government Response to Offshore Oil Development: The Experience of Santa Barbara County Government." Paper presented to the annual meeting of the American Political Science Association, San Francisco, August 30–September 2.

Lineberry, Robert and Edmund Fowler. 1967. " Reformism and Public Policies in American Cities." *American Political Science Review* 61: 701–716.

Logan, John R. and Harvey L. Molotch. 1987. *Urban Fortunes: The Political Economy of Place*. Berkeley: University of California Press.

Logan, John R. and Mark Schneider. 1984. "Racial Segregation and Racial Change in American Suburbs, 1970–1980." *American Journal of Sociology* 89: 874–888.

Loomis, Charles P. and J. Allan Beegle. 1975. *A Strategy for Rural Change*. New York: Schenkman.

Mack, Connie. 1992. "Remarks." *Congressional Record—Senate*. (March 12): S3490–91.

MacManus, Susan A. and William J. Pammer Jr. 1990. "Cutbacks in the County: Retrenchment in Rural Villages, Townships, and Counties." *Public Administration Quarterly* 14 (Fall): 302– 323.

Malone, Claude, D. 1986. "The County Administrator: Complexity at the New Frontier." *Public Management* (October): 4–6.

Mann, S. Z., and R. M. Stout. 1963. "The Broome County Airport." In Robert T. Frost, ed., *Cases in State and Local Government*. Englewood Cliffs, N.J.: Prentice-Hall, 321–336.

Manning, R. D. 1988. "How Three Women Took Over Missoula County and the 'Gender Factor' Became an Edge." *Governing* 1(8): 44–50.

Marando, Vincent L. and Mavis Mann Reeves. 1990. "County Government Structure: Influence of State and Region." Paper delivered at the Annual Meeting of the American Political Science Association, San Francisco, August 30–September 2.

_____ . 1991. "Counties: Evolving Local Governments, Reform and Responsiveness." *National Civic Review* 80 (Spring): 222–226.

Marando, Vincent L. and Robert D. Thomas. 1977. *The Forgotten Governments: County Commissioners as Policy Makers*. Gainesville: The University Presses of Florida.

Martin, Lawrence L. 1991. "An Assessment of Actual Versus Potential County Discretionary Authority." *Southeastern Political Review* (forthcoming).

Martin, Linda, ed. 1984. *Local Government Autonomy in California*. Davis: Institute of Governmental Affairs, University of California.

Martin, Roscoe C., Frank J. Munger, J. Burkhead, and G. S. Birkhead. 1965. *Decisions in Syracuse*. Garden City, N.Y.: Anchor Books.

Mason, Bruce B. and Heinz R. Hink. 1982. *Constitutional Government in Arizona*. Tempe, Ariz.: Cleber Publishing Company.

Meier, George. 1991. "State Becoming a Vast Suburb." *St. Petersburg Times* (February 16): B1.

Miles, Rufus E. 1978. "The Origin and Meaning of Miles' Law." *Public Administration Review* 38 (September/October): 399–403.

Mladenka, K. R. and K. Q. Hill. 1989. *Texas Government: Politics and Economics*. Pacific Grove, Calif.: Brooks-Cole.

Morgan, David R. and Michael W. Hirlinger. 1991. "Intergovernmental Service Contracts: A Multivariate Explanation." *Urban Affairs Quarterly* 27 (September): 128– 144.

Murphy, Thomas P. and J. Rehfuss. 1976. *Urban Politics in the Suburban Era*. Homewood, Ill.: Dorsey Press.

Nalbandian, John. 1990. "Tenets of Contemporary Professionalism in Local Government." *Public Administration Review* (November/December): 654–662.

National Association of Counties (NACo). 1990. *The American County Platform and Resolutions*. Washington, D.C.: NACo.

_____ . 1991. *State-Local Report*. Washington, D.C.: NACo.

National Conference of State Legislatures (NCSL). 1989. *State-Local Task Force*. Denver: NCSL.

Nice, David C. 1987. *Federalism: The Politics of Intergovernmental Relations*. New York: St. Martin's Press.

Norris, Michele L. 1991. "Bill for '80s Comes Due in Montgomery, PG." *Washington Post* (August 31): B1, B5.

Oakerson, Ronald J., Roger B. Parks, and H. A. Bell. 1987. "How Fragmentation Works—St. Louis Style." Paper presented at the Midwest Political Science Association Meeting, Chicago.

Office of Technology Assessment, Congress of the United States. 1991. *Rural America at the Crossroads: Networking for the Future*. Washington, D.C.: U.S. Government Printing Office.

Ostrowski, John W., Louise G. White, and John D.R. Cole. 1984. "Local Government Capacity Building: A Structured Group Process Approach." *Administration and Society* 16 (May): 3–26.

Parks, Roger B. 1991. "Counties in the Federal System: The Interlocal Connection." *Intergovernmental Perspective* 17 (Winter): 29–32.

Peterson, Paul. 1981. *City Limits*. Chicago: University of Chicago Press.

Poister, Theodore H. and Gregory Streib. 1989. "Management Tools in Municipal Government: Trends Over the Last Decade."*Public Administration Review* 49: 240–248.

Rapp, David. 1989. "The Federal Government is Still the Only Game in Town When Farmers Need Help." *Governing* (April): 23–27.

Reed, B. J. 1983. "The Changing Role of Local Advocacy in National Politics." *Journal of Urban Affairs* 5 (Fall): 287–298.

Reeder, Richard J. 1990. "Introduction." In *Local Revenue Diversification: Rural Economies*. Washington, D.C.: Advisory Commission on Intergovernmental Relations, Report SR-13 (March): 1–5.

Renner, Tari. 1988. "Municipal Election Processes: The Impact on Minority Representation." In *The Municipal Year Book 1988*. Washington, D.C.: International City Management Association.

Richter, Kerry. 1985. "Nonmetropolitan Growth in the Late 1970s: The End of the Turnaround?" *Demography* (May): 245–263.

Rymarowicz, Lillian and Dennis Zimmerman. 1988. *Federal Budget and Tax Policy and the State-Local Sector: Retrenchment in the 1980s*. Washington, D.C.: Congressional Research Service (September 9).

Salant, Priscilla. 1990. *A Community Researcher's Guide to Rural Data*. Washington, D.C.: Island Press and the Rural Economic Policy Program of the Aspen Institute.

Salant, Tanis J. 1988a. *County Home Rule: Perspectives for Decision-Making in Arizona*. Tucson: Office of Community and Public Service, University of Arizona.

_____. 1988b. "County Home Rule: Challenging the Tenets of Reform." DPA dissertation. Sacramento: Public Affairs Center, University of Southern California.

_____. 1989. *Arizona County Government: A Study of Contemporary Issues*. Tucson: Office of Community and Public Service, University of Arizona.

_____. 1991. "County Governments: An Overview." *Intergovernmental Perspective* 17 (Winter): 5–9.

Schneider, Mark and Kee Ok Park. 1989. "Metropolitan Counties as Service Delivery Agents: The Still Forgotten Governments." *Public Administration Review* 49 (July/August): 345–352.

Scholl, T. W. 1963. "A College for Jefferson County?" In Richard T. Frost, ed., *Cases in State and Local Government*. Englewood Cliffs, N.J.: Prentice-Hall.

Seroka, Jim. 1988. "Community Growth and Administrative Capacity." *National Civic Review* (January/February): 42–46.

Shanahan, Eileen. 1991. "Going it Jointly: Regional Solutions for Local Problems." *Governing* (August): 70–75.

Sharp, Elaine B. 1990. *Urban Politics and Administration: From Service Delivery to Economic Development*. New York: Longman.

Snider, Clyde F. 1952. "American County Government: A Mid-Century Review." *American Political Science Review* (March): 66–80.

_____. 1957. *Local Government in Rural America*. New York: Appelton-Century-Crofts.

Sokolow, Alvin D. 1964. "Folk Society Politics: Conflict and Organization in Two Rural Illinois Counties." Ph.D. dissertation. University of Illinois, Urbana.

_____. 1984. "The Elected Official as Expert: Governing Boards in Rural Communities." *Rural Development Perspectives* 1: 4–9.

_____. 1986. "Management without the Manager: The Administrative Work of Legislators in Rural Local Government." In Jim Seroka, ed., *Rural Public Administration: Problems and Prospects*. Westport, Conn.: Greenwood Press, 59–75.

_____. 1987. "Legislators without Ambition: Recruiting Citizens to Small Town Office." Paper presented to the Annual Meeting of the American Political Science Association. Chicago, September 3–6.

Stanfield, Rochelle L. 1976. "The PIGs: Out of the Sty, Into Lobbying with Style." *National Journal* (August 14): 228–233.

Stewart, D. Michael. 1991. "Counties in the Federal System: The Washington Connection." *Intergovernmental Perspective* 17 (Winter): 18–20.

Stewart, Jill. 1990. "Census Figures Paint a Checkered Portrait." *Los Angeles Times* (August 29): B1, B4.

Stinson, Thomas F. 1990. "Local Revenue Diversification: Implications for Nonmetropolitan Communities." In *Local Revenue Diversification; Rural Economies*. Washington, D.C.: Advisory Commission on Intergovernmental Relations, Report SR-13 (March): 67–85.

Streib, Gregory and Theodore H. Poister. 1989. "New Tools for New Challenges: A Twelve-Year Perspective on the Use of Municipal Management Tools." In *The Municipal Year Book 1989*. Washington, D.C.: International City Management Association.

Streib, Gregory and William L. Waugh. Jr. 1990. "Assessing County Officials' Perspectives on Intergovernmental Relations and Local Capacity." Paper presented at the Annual Meeting of the American Political Science Association, San Francisco, August 30–September 2.

_____. 1991a. "County Administrative Capacity and the Barriers to Effective Management." *Public Productivity and Management Review* 15 (Fall):61–70.

_____. 1991b. "The Changing Responsibilities of County Governments." *American Review of Public Administration* 21 (June): 139–155.

_____. 1991c. "Probing the Limits of County Reform in an Era of Scarcity." *Public Administration Quarterly* (forthcoming).

"Survey forecasts gloomy budget outlook for the states." 1991. *Tucson Citizen* (August 13).

Svara, J. 1990. *Official Leadership in the City: Patterns of Conflict.* New York: Oxford University Press.

Sylvester, Kathleen. 1989. "The Mandate Blues." *Governing* (September): 26–30.

Thomas, John. 1987. "A Perspective on County Government Services and Financing." *State and Local Government Review* (Fall): 119–121.

Thomas, Robert D. 1991. "Counties in Transition: Issues and Challenges." *Intergovernmental Perspective* 17 (Winter): 41–44.

Todd, Barbara. 1991. " Counties in the Federal System: The State Connection." *Intergovernmental Perspective* 17 (Winter): 21–25.

Torrence, Susan Walker. 1974. *Grass Roots Government: The County in American Politics.* New York: Robert B. Luce. Inc.

U.S. Advisory Commission on Intergovernmental Relations (ACIR). 1972. *Profile of County Government.* Washington, D.C.: U.S. Government Printing Office.

_____. 1981. *Measuring Local Discretionary Authority.* Washington, D.C.: U.S. Government Printing Office.

_____. 1982. *State and Local Roles in the Federal System.* Washington, D.C.: U.S. Government Printing Office.

_____. 1990. *Mandates: Cases In State-Local Relations.* Washington, D.C.: U.S. Government Printing Office.

_____. 1991. *Changing Public Attitudes on Government and Taxes.* Washington, D.C.: U.S. Government Printing Office.

U.S. Bureau of the Census. 1988. "Government Organization." *1987 Census of Governments.* Washington, D.C.: U.S. Government Printing Office.

_____. 1990. "Finances of County Governments." *1987 Census of Governments.* Washington, D.C.: U.S. Government Printing Office.

U.S. Department of Agriculture. 1987. *Rural Economic Development in the 1980s: A Summary.* Washington, D.C.: U.S. Department of Agriculture.

_____. 1988. *Rural Economic Development in the 1980s: Prospects for the Future.* Washington, D.C.: US Department of Agriculture.

_____. 1989. *A Hard Look at USDA's Rural Development Programs.* Washington, D.C.: U.S. Department of Agriculture.

U.S. Department of Commerce. 1989. *Rural and Rural Farm Population: 1988.* Washington, D.C.: Bureau of the Census, 1989.

U.S. General Accounting Office (GAO). 1989. *Rural Development: Federal Programs that Focus on Rural America and Its Economic Development.*

Washington, D.C.: U.S. General Accounting Office, GAO/RCED-56BR (January).

Van Petten, Donald Robinson. 1956. *The Constitution and Government of Arizona*. Phoenix: Sun Country Publishing Company.

Vobejda, Barbara. 1990. "Census Quantifies Trouble in Heartland, Growth on the Coasts." *The Washington Post* (September 3): A6.

Wager, Paul W., ed. 1950. *County Government Across the Nation*. Chapel Hill: University of North Carolina Press.

Walker, David B. 1986. "Intergovernmental Relations and the Well-Governed City: Cooperation, Confrontation, Clarification." *National Civic Review* (March-April): 65–87.

Walters, Johnathan. 1991. "Lobbying for the Good Old Days." *Governing* (June): 33–37.

Ward, Janet. 1992. "Can Two Live As Cheaply As One?" *American City and County* (February): 30–36.

Waugh, William L., Jr. 1976. *County Home Rule Experience in the U.S*. Office of Public Service and Research, Auburn University.

_____. 1988. "States, Counties, and the Questions of Trust and Capacity." *Publius: The Journal of Federalism* 18: 189–198.

Waugh, William L., Jr. and Ronald John Hy. 1988, "The Administrative, Fiscal, and Political Capacities of County Governments." *State and Local Government Review* 20: 28–31.

Waugh, William L., Jr. and Gregory Streib. 1989. "An Uneasy Partnership: County Officials and Trust in the States." Paper presented to the Annual Meeting of the American Society for Public Administration, Miami.

_____. 1990. "County Officials' Perceptions of Local Capacity and State Responsiveness After the First Reagan Term." *Southeastern Political Review* 18 (Spring): 27–50.

Weaver, Kenneth L. 1992. "Rural County Government Reform: The Montana Case." Paper prepared for the Annual Meeting of the Western Political Science Association. San Francisco.

Webb, Sidney and Beatrice Webb. 1906. *English Local Government from the Revolution to the Municipal Corporation Act: The Parish and the County*. London: Longmans, Green and Co.

Weinberg, Mark. 1984. "Budget Retrenchment in Small Cities: A Comparative Analysis of Wooster and Athens, Ohio." *Public Budgeting & Finance* 4: 46–57.

Wenum, J. D. 1991. *Introduction to County Government: Guidelines for County Board Members*. Urbana: Community Information and Education Service, University of Illinois.

Wilson, D. and A. H. Elder. 1987. "Collective Bargaining in Illinois Counties." In R. P. Wolensky and E. J. Miller, eds., *The Small City and Regional Community*, Vol. 7. Stevens Point: University of Wisconsin, 86–91.

Wright, Deil S. 1988. *Understanding Intergovernmental Relations*. Pacific Grove, CA: Brooks/Cole Publishing Company.

Zeller, Florence. 1975. "Forms of County Government." *The County Year-book—1975*. Washington, D.C.: National Association of Counties and International City Management Association.

Zimmerman, Joseph F. 1981. *Measuring Local Discretionary Authority*. Washington, D.C.: Advisory Commission on Intergovernmental Relations, M-131, November.

_____. 1983. *State-Local Relations: A Partnership Approach*. New York: Praeger.

_____. 1990. "Alternative Local Electoral Systems." *National Civic Review* 79 (January–February): 23–36.

Index

About the Contributors

C. DOUGLAS BAKER is a local government staff specialist at the Institute of Governmental Services, University of Maryland, where he is also a graduate student in the Department of Government and Politics.

J. EDWIN BENTON is an Associate Professor in the Department of Government and International Relations at the University of South Florida. He is the author of several studies on county government and is coeditor of *Intergovernmental Relations and Public Policy* (1986).

DAVID R. BERMAN is a Professor of Political Science at Arizona State University, where he specializes in state and local government, politics, and public policy. He has published several books, book chapters, and journal articles in these areas.

BEVERLY A. CIGLER is a Professor of Public Policy and Administration at Penn State University, Harrisburg. She is the author of over 60 journal articles, book chapters, and technical reports, and two team-authored books. Dr. Cigler's research interests are broadly concerned with the politics, management, and policies of local and state governments.

VICTOR S. DESANTIS is an Assistant Professor of Public Administration at the University of North Texas. He is the author of "County Government: A Century of Change," in the 1989 *Municipal Year Book*, and several other papers and articles relating to county government.

BARBARA P. GREENE is a Professor of Political Science at Central Michigan University. She has worked closely with the National Association of Counties and has published on county government and finances.

KATHERYN A. LEHMAN is in the Ph.D. program at Arizona State University, specializing in state and local politics. She has presented papers at meetings of the American Political Science Association and recently coauthored a chapter in *Governors and Hard Times*.

VINCENT L. MARANDO is Professor of Government and Politics at the University of Maryland, College Park. He was written two books and numerous articles on county government, and is currently working on a book dealing with county agenda setting.

LAWRENCE L. MARTIN is an Assistant Professor of Public Administration at Florida Atlantic University in Boca Raton. He has written books and numerous articles on state and local government. He served for several years as Director, Office of Management Analysis, Maricopa County Government, Phoenix, Arizona.

DONALD C. MENZEL is Professor of Public Administration in the Department of Government and International Relations at the University of South Florida. His current research interests include organizational ethics in local government, intergovernmental policy implementation, and governance issues in urban counties.

TARI RENNER is an Assistant Professor in the Department of Political Science, Duquesne University, Pittsburgh. He has specialized in the area of local election systems.

TANIS J. SALANT is a Senior Research Specialist for the Office of Community and Public Service at the University of Arizona, where she coordinates the Division of Government Programs. She has published numerous books and articles on county government including a national study on the shifting roles in county-state relations.

ALVIN D. SOKOLOW is a public policy specialist with the Cooperative Extension Service of the University of California. He was a Professor of Political Science at the University's Davis campus for 27 years. His research and extension activities are focused on government, politics, and policy in small communities. He is the author of numerous books and articles dealing with local government.

GREGORY STREIB is Assistant Professor of Public Administration in the School of Public Administration and Urban Studies at Georgia State University. He has published numerous articles and book chapters on local government management.

WILLIAM L. WAUGH, JR. is a Professor of Public Administration and Political Science and acting Director of the School of Public Administration and Urban Studies at Georgia State University. Among his published works are several articles on county-state relations.